GREAT RAILROAD MUSEUMS OF THE USA

Jan B Young

GREAT RAILROAD MUSEUMS OF THE USA

JAN B YOUNG

ISBN 978-1-300-75555-5

Above: Milwaukee Road 118C gets a bath outside the engine house at the Illinois Railway Museum in 1989. The unit is an EMD F7A built in 1951.

The cover: Nevada Northern number 93 in the engine house in Ely, Nevada in 2012. This 2-8-0 locomotive is a 1909 product of Alco's Pittsburgh Works.

CARS AND TRAINS

Studebaker and the Railroads
A two volume history of the Studebaker Corporation of South Bend, Indiana, railroading in the South Bend area, and connections between them

Tales of Studebaker: The Early Years
Historic sidelights and illuminating stories about the company and the people

History of the American Automobile Industry
Reprint of a 1916 history by the editor of *The Automobile*, David Beecroft

The Studebaker History Corner
More than a hundred short historic stories about Studebaker

Studebaker Bibliography
A catalog of almost five thousand books and articles about Studebaker

History of the Studebaker Corporation
Reprint of a rare 1918 book by Albert Erskine, Studebaker's President

TW and ASR Indexes
Indexes of the content of Turning Wheels and Antique Studebaker Review magazines

The Life of Clement Studebaker
Reprint of a biography believed to have been written by Ann Studebaker after his death

FICTION

Mom and Me
Three novellas prominently featuring cats

Claude
A novel of the distant future

Eternity
A novel of heaven and happenings in the afterlife

Nothing Personal
A parking garage mugging leads to incredible consequences

TRAVEL

Atlantic Coast by RV
2011 travel through Alabama to Georgia and the Carolinas in full color

Northwest USA by RV
Our 2010 travel to Oregon and Washington with lots of other stops, all in full color

Missouri and Maine by RV
Two separate trips in 2009, one to Missouri and one to Maine in full color

Alaska by RV
Our 2008 trip to Alaska, western Canada and the northwestern USA in color

LOGISTICS

Best Practices in Replenishment of Forward Pick Locations
Options for replenishment and how to choose the best methods

Choosing and Using a Consultant
Finding a consultant who will actually be worth your time and money

Cycle Count and Physical Inventory Design and Execution
Designing and operating efficient and effective methods

Designing and Using Carousels in the Warehouse
Analyzing operations to design the optimum carousel installation

Selecting, Buying, Installing and Using a Modern Warehouse Management System
The title says it all

Simulation in the Supply Chain
What simulation technology can and cannot do in the supply chain

Supply Chain Metrics
How to measure and monitor supply chain operations

GENERAL INTEREST

State Flags of the United States
Images, symbolism and history of the US state and territorial flags in full color

The United States Constitution
The history and content of the US Constitution and all its amendments

Thirty Years as a Volunteer Treasurer
What I learned in thirty years as a church treasurer

Our Ancestry
A three volume set listing almost twelve thousand people and their relationships

The Assassins
Forty-six historic stories of murder and mayhem on a global scale

Personal Finance
My take on how to save, borrow, invest, spend and meet your goals.

CONTENTS

The Glamour of the Railroads

Although it may be hard for us to understand today, in the early days of railroading and especially in the years after completion of the transcontinental railroad, almost everyone looked on the new technology of overland steam travel with awe and admiration. The desire to be a locomotive engineer wasn't limited to small boys, but spread through a good portion of the male population and doubtless into the secret hearts of some of the female population as well.

The railroads had their detractors, primarily people whose livelihood depended on low freight rates, but their enmity was mostly directed at railroad management and less at the men who ran the trains or at the trains themselves. Long distance travel by rail became a goal that a person would work for and look forward to for years before finally achieving it. And even into the 1920s, the romance remained. The depot was the place to see and be seen. Locomotives and cars were studied and their relative advantages became the subject of barroom discussion and even the occasional fistfight. And the introduction of new equipment or the completion of a new rail line brought instant attention from the public and the press along with further discussion.

An entire generation – or even two – was brought up understanding that the steam locomotive was the pinnacle of technology. Toys based on railroad subjects became highly popular as young boys dreamt of their future in the right-hand seat and young girls hoped to marry a railroad man and settle down to a life of security in a railroad town. The fact that reality was markedly different from the dreams made no difference. The railroads were romantic and stayed that way for a very long time.

Glamour and romance, like deep and narrow rock canyons, have long-lasting echoes. While the automobile and the airplane eventually replaced the train as a means of practical personal travel, they never succeeded in stealing away the romance and if we listen carefully, we can still hear those echoes from the past. And the fact is that the echoes can best be heard in the presence of physical reminders like antique locomotives, ancient wood-framed passenger cars, and other bits of still existing railroadiana. This is why I love railroad museums and why I am joined by so many others.

If a census were to be taken (and this book is not such a census), I think even confirmed railfans like myself would be surprised by the amount of historic equipment that has been saved and by the number of organizations in this country dedicated to preserving, restoring, and sometimes operating it. In total, the museums listed in this book hold more than five thousand locomotives and cars and occupy about two square miles of land.

Further, I think we would be amazed at the number of people who come out every year to gape, even if they have no deep knowledge of what they're gaping at. I have a list of more than six hundred railroad-related attractions in North America and I'm sure it isn't complete. The list includes everything from the fascinating to the trivial, from the huge to the tiny, and from the significant rail yard to the modest depot museum, but its length alone reflects our interest in trains and railroading. There are museums

Railroad Magazine was published monthly from 1906 to 1979 (with interruptions and name changes). Printed on the cheapest pulp paper and bound almost casually, it featured color covers that epitomized the romance of the rails. The one shown here is from the January 1938 issue.

devoted to automobiles, trucks, airplanes and boats, but not more than are devoted to the rails.

The fact that I am old enough to remember seeing actual, working steam locomotives contributes to my attitude, but I hope I have passed some of my enthusiasm down the next generation, even though they will probably never be thrilled at the chance to see the one remaining Pennsylvania P-5 electric in St. Louis and even get a chance to pat its flank. I blush to say that I was. And that goes for the Espee cab-forward that lives in Sacramento, the John Bull in Washington (although flank-patting is forbidden in the Smithsonian), and the two remaining UP turbines, one near Chicago and the other in Ogden.

I've traveled a lot, especially since I retired. While I haven't visited every railroad museum in the United States, I've seen many of them and I've seen essentially all the ones reputed to be important. Although there are other books on the subject of railroad museums, I thought one that gave even an admittedly biased rating to the very best and brought the top museums on the continent to the attention of railfan readers would be useful. That's what I've tried to do here. If you've been to all the museums listed in this book, you've seen the best. If you haven't, I hope my descriptions provide some guidance when you have an opportunity to travel and see more of them.

About This Book

This book is neither a catalog nor a definitive study. It is, rather, a reflection of my experiences and opinions backed up by research and contact with the various museums.

My objective in writing this book has been to pass along what I've learned and also to indirectly promote visits to these and other railroad museums. Visits translate into cash for the museums and that cash translates into additional acquisitions and additional preservation. Thus I do my bit to save these historic dinosaurs.

So what makes a great railroad museum? I think there are six criteria. To be "great" a museum must rate highly in at least four and acceptably in the other two.

- Size. Size can be measured in acres of land, feet of track, number of pieces of equipment, number of locomotives or several other ways. The details are less important than is the fact that size does matter. The single locomotive in a park can be of real interest, but can never constitute a "great" railroad museum.

- Rarity. A thousand acres packed with ten thousand recently retired railgons does not constitute a "great" museum. At least one and preferably several pieces of equipment should be one-of-a-kind, only-remaining, or at least unusual, and should also be historically significant.

- Antiquity. Lots of railroad museums have lightweight passenger cars; they were cast off by the hundreds after Amtrak took its pick of the fleet in 1971. A "great" railroad museum has at least one and preferably several pieces that date from World War I or earlier and at least one and preferably several pieces that date prior to 1890. Reproductions don't count except for the very few that are, themselves, so old they qualify.

- Quality and Preservation. Back lots full of rusting junk are fun to see and actually are one of the things I look for when I visit railroad museums. But the "great" museums have restored at least some of their equipment, have made a few pieces operational, and are maintaining and improving their level of quality and restoration as time goes on.

- Scope. The greatest railroad museums are not limited in scope. They include equipment from a number of railroads and preferably from a number of major regions around the country. They include steam, diesel and electric railroad locomotives and cars, standard and narrow-gauge equipment, plus interurbans, streetcars and rapid transit equipment. Truly broad scope also includes the collection and display of railroad-related items other than rolling stock.

- Presentation. To be "great", the museum must make its collection accessible to the visitor. Accessibility, as I define it, is difficult to achieve while still meeting preservation goals. Many museums have significant and interesting equipment stored in dark barns or weedy rail yards, crammed together with other equipment so closely that, although one can see and even touch the pieces, one cannot see and photograph an entire piece at one time.

An example that tugs at my heart is the Reuben Wells, an ancient and historic 0-10-0 steam locomotive that has long been at the Children's Museum in Indianapolis. While it is easy to visit and see the locomotive, it is displayed in such a way that it's impossible to get an overall view and thus impossible to get a feel for what the locomotive really looked like when it was operational. At the opposite end of the spectrum is the John Bull, displayed by the Smithsonian in a spacious, well-lit room where it is protected from both the elements and the visitors but still easily visible to all.

Good presentation also requires that some attention be paid to visitor amenities: weeds need to be cut, paths maintained, rest rooms cleaned and, most important, exhibits need to be labeled so visitors know what they're looking at.

This book, by the way, ignores railroad museums that do not include full-size, prototype rolling stock. No matter how many timetables and uniforms and how much china is displayed, such a museum cannot be "great". It also ignores museums that do not display their collection and only operate train rides or dinner trains – except for a few, listed in a separate chapter in the back. I can only stand so many murder mysteries and so many phony train robberies. While it's important to involve and educate younger generations, Thomas the Tank Engine is not aimed at me or my peers.

This book also ignores museums based on small-gauge park railroads, live steam clubs or small-scale model railroad layouts. While there is a great deal of fascination in modeling, and while many of the builders of live steam locomotives and model layouts have achieved awesome things, they are in an entirely different class and are not considered here.

In many cases, classification of the museums wasn't easy and I struggled to devise a consistent and sensible way of doing it. Hopefully I succeeded. Within the classes (really great, great, really good, and good), the museums are listed in zip code order, roughly east to west across the country.

There are a lot of railroad museums – hundreds – in this country that haven't rated mention. They fact that these museums didn't achieve "good" status in my evaluation doesn't mean they are "bad," it just means that they are small and have little or nothing that is remarkable from the railfan's viewpoint. Many have only one or two pieces of on-rail equipment and some have none. My classification is most certainly not intended to denigrate the often considerable efforts put in by the volunteers who run these museums.

Museums come and go and, in particular, equipment sometimes moves from museum to museum. Museums also move equipment into and out of storage and into and out of restoration shops where it may be inaccessible at times. The information in this book was correct to the best of my knowledge as of the end of 2012, but if you're especially interested in a particular item or a particular museum, it's wise to call ahead.

The statistics I present are not always precise. Addresses given are physical addresses and may not be appropriate if you wish to mail something to a museum. Please consult museum web sites for mailing addresses.

For many of the museums in this book the reader will notice a "visit suggestion," either morning, afternoon, or mid-day. I have visited museums too many times to find that I was there at the wrong time to day to get the best sun angle on the displays and thus my photography suffered. The suggestions in this book won't solve all photography problems on all pieces in all museums, but hopefully they will help.

Another suggestion: when you visit one of these museums, particularly the non-profit ones, pay the admission fee but also make a donation (or at least buy something in the gift shop). These organizations need our support if they are to last into the future.

Finally, by way of disclosure I should mention that I have long been a member of the Illinois Railway Museum because it is so fascinating and because I live about a hundred miles from it. I admit to a mild bias, but believe that my evaluation of it would be supported by many other railfans. I have no other museum connections and have received no consideration from any museum for inclusion in this book. The commentary is my own, carrying no biases but mine. Errors, likewise, are mine.

Map of the Museums

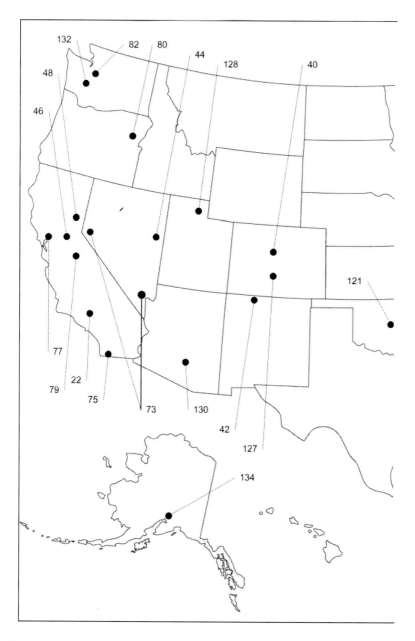

Great Railroad Museums of the USA

Reference numbers on the map below refer to page numbers in this book.

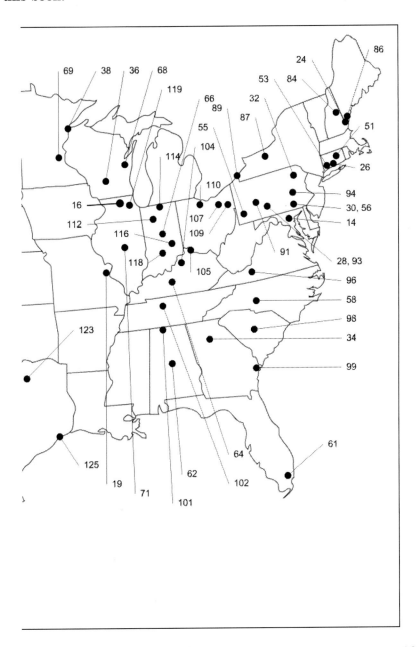

The Really Great Museums

What I consider the really great railroad museums are the ones I would plan a trip of a thousand miles to visit and would go back to (and have gone back to) time after time. They are museums where I won't go if I have only two hours to spend because I know at the end of that time I'll be only part way through and will greatly regret having to leave.

There are four really great museums in the United States. Listed in zip code order, they are:

B&O Railway Museum, Baltimore, MD

901 West Pratt Street
Baltimore, MD 21223
(410) 752-2490
www.borail.org

Size	Rarity	Antiquity	Quality	Scope	Presentation
A	A+	A	A	B	A

Land Area	**40 Acres**
Dates From	**1953**
Gauge	**Standard**
Ownership	**Private, Non-profit**
Visit Suggestion	**Morning**
Track	**1 Mile**
Locomotives	**22 Steam** **18 Diesel** **3 Electric** **1 Other**
Rolling stock	**14 Passenger** **13 Freight** **7 Nonrevenue**

The Baltimore & Ohio Railway Museum achieves "really great" status by virtue of the antiquity and the state of preservation of its holdings. While the B&O Museum isn't small, it lives on urban land and is thus hedged in and unable to grow.

Chesapeake & Ohio 490 was built as a 4-6-2 Pacific by Alco in 1926, but shortly after World War II, the C&O converted it along with four sister Pacifics, making them 4-6-4 Hudsons. Streamlining was applied at the time of the conversion.

The B&O Railway Museum originated with the historic collection of the Baltimore & Ohio Railroad. The B&O had preserved selected pieces of equipment since 1876 and when the Mt. Claire passenger car shop was closed, the railroad moved all of its historic equipment there and, in 1953, opened the museum under railroad ownership. In 1990 the CSX Corporation, successor to the B&O and other railroads, donated the shops, the land and the collection to a new, independent museum corporation. After a major roof collapse in 2003 caused by excessive snow, the building was rebuilt and it again houses the most valuable pieces in the collection.

The list of historic artifacts held by the museum is far too long to include more than just a sampling in this book, but of special note are:

- The Atlantic, a grasshopper type 0-4-0 built in 1832 in the B&O shops. (The locomotive on display is actually a replica. Historic in its own right, it was built in 1892 by Ross Winans.)
- The Pioneer, a 2-2-2T built in 1851 by Seth Wilmarth for the Cumberland Valley Railroad
- The Tom Thumb, a replica of the original built in 1926 by the Baltimore & Ohio

- The William Mason, an American type 4-4-0 built in 1856 by the Mason Machine Works
- The A J Cromwell, a Consolidation type 2-8-0 built in 1888 by the Baltimore & Ohio
- Chesapeake & Ohio 1604, an Allegheny type 2-6-6-6 built by Lima Locomotive Works in 1941
- Chesapeake & Ohio 490, a Hudson type 4-6-4 built in 1926 by the American Locomotive Company, displayed with streamlining in place
- Baltimore & Ohio 1961, a Budd-built RDC diesel powered passenger car
- Central of New Jersey 1000, a box-cab diesel switcher built by Alco/GE in 1925. It was the first commercially successful diesel-electric
- Baltimore & Ohio 10, a 1909 box-cab electric locomotive built by General Electric

In addition, the museum includes a very rare Baltimore & Ohio wagon-top box car, two 1883 iron pot hopper cars, a Bethlehem Steel hot metal car, and other freight equipment and passenger cars dating back as far as 1868.

The B&O Railway Museum also holds and displays collections of clocks, pocket watches, lanterns, dining car china and silver, fine art, communication devices, signals, shop equipment, and tools.

Illinois Railway Museum, Union, IL

7000 Olson Rd
Union, IL 60180
(815) 923-4000
www.irm.org

Size	Rarity	Antiquity	Quality	Scope	Presentation
A+	A	A	A	A+	A

Land Area	97 Acres
Dates From	1953
Gauge	Standard
Ownership	Private, non-profit
Visit Suggestion	Afternoon
Track	5 Miles
Locomotives	25 Steam 44 Diesel 14 Electric 3 Other
Rolling stock	70 Passenger 90 Freight 31 Nonrevenue 94 Traction

The Illinois Railway Museum is located close to Chicago, which could be the one point in the United States most connected to the railways.
Throughout railroad history, Chicago has always been the primary

Union Pacific gas turbine number 18 at the Illinois Railway Museum.

and most important meeting point of eastern and western lines. In part because of this geography, and in part because the museum has always had dedicated and excellent management and many, many volunteers, it is probably the greatest railroad museum in the world.

Certainly in terms of size and diversity, the Illinois Railway Museum is hard to beat. The collection includes steam, diesel and electric and both western and eastern equipment. Included in the electric department are streetcars, interurbans, heavy electric locomotives, and rapid transit cars. Steam and diesel locomotives span the country from Union Pacific and Atchison, To-

peka & Santa Fe to Norfolk & Western and Louisville & Nashville. In terms of diversity, the only shortcoming of the Illinois
Railway Museum is a lack of significant narrow-gauge equipment.

The Illinois Railway Museum was started in 1953 with the effort
to save a single interurban car, but expanded greatly. The museum moved from downtown Chicago to its present site in 1964
and has since continued to buy surrounding land as it comes
available to provide buffer space against encroaching development.

Important pieces of equipment at the Illinois Railway Museum
include:
- Chicago, North Shore & Milwaukee number 801-802, an
  "Electroliner," one of only two ever made.
- An 1859 North Chicago Street Railroad horse car
- A 1934 Chicago Surface Lines cable car
- Illinois Terminal number 234 and 504, respectively, a very
  rare interurban observation car and even rarer sleeper
- Pennsylvania Railroad GG-1 number 4927 (Amtrak 4939)
- Chicago, South Shore & South Bend 803 (a "Little Joe")
- Norfolk & Western number 2050, a 1923 2-8-8-2 class Y3a
- Chicago, Milwaukee, St. Paul & Pacific number 265, a 1944
  4-8-4 Northern
- Atchison, Topeka & Santa Fe number 2903, a 1943 4-8-4
  Northern
- Union Pacific number 18, one of two still-existing UP gas
  turbines
- Delaware Lackawanna & Western number 3001, a 1926 Al-
  co/GE boxcab diesel
- Minneapolis Northfield & Southern Railway 21, a Baldwin
  DT6-6-2000 center cab, the only surviving Baldwin center
  cab locomotive.
- The Nebraska Zephyr, an almost complete 5-car CB&Q
  streamlined train (including rib-sided diesel number 9911,
  the only surviving EMD E5A), restored and operational.
- Baltimore & Ohio number 374065, a wagon-top boxcar
- Borden's number 520 a stream-styled milk tanker, also
  known as a butter-dish car.

The Illinois Railway Museum also has an operating collection of trolley buses (overhead wires and rubber tires), a collection of railway signals wired for demonstration operation and a research library that includes the Pullman Archives.

Museum of Transportation, St. Louis, MO

2967 Barrett Station Rd
St. Louis, MO 63122
(314) 965-7998
transportmuseumassociation.org

Size	Rarity	Antiquity	Quality	Scope	Presentation
A+	A+	A+	A	A+	A

Land Area	129 Acres
Dates From	1944
Gauge	Standard
Ownership	Public
Visit Suggestion	Morning
Locomotives	32 Steam
	20 Diesel
	8 Electric
	7 Other
Rolling Stock	26 Passenger
	41 Freight
	15 Nonrevenue
	29 Traction

If Chicago is the point in the USA most connected to the railroads, St. Louis is second. Historically more than twenty railroads met in the city where the Museum of Transportation now lies. This made St. Louis a major transportation hub and an important center of railroading.

The Museum of Transportation was founded in 1944 with the purchase of a mule-drawn streetcar, the "Bellefontaine." The initial group found interest in the community, so they incorporated in 1948 and acquired the land the museum now sits on.

Milwaukee Road bipolar number E-2, a heavy electric locomotive designed primarily for passenger service on the Milwaukee Road's Coast Division.

From its earliest days, Purdue University (West Lafayette, Indiana) taught railway engineering and economics and gained the nickname "boilermakers" as a result. Purdue gathered locomotive donations from a number of sources as an adjunct to its classwork and, at least at one point, considered the possibility of opening a railroad museum. When Purdue finally began to disperse its collection, by then including some ancient and historic pieces, a significant share went to the Museum of Transportation in St. Louis. This increased the museum's presence and brought it a measure of fame among railfans.

In 1979, the volunteer organization that had created the museum donated it to St. Louis County, which continues to own and operate it today.

Holdings include:
- The Daniel Nason, a 4-4-0 locomotive built by the Boston & Providence in 1858
- A four-wheel, stagecoach-style passenger car built in 1833 by the Boston & Providence. It is the oldest American passenger railroad car in existence.
- The Charles H, a Lake Street Elevated (Chicago) 0-4-4T Forney-type built by the Rhode Island Locomotive Works in 1893
- DL&W number 952 a 4-4-0 "camelback" built in 1905 by Alco

- Union Pacific Centennial number 6944 built in 1971 by EMD
- Baltimore & Ohio number 50, the first long-distance passenger diesel put in service in the USA, built in 1935 by General Motors/General Electric
- Milwaukee Road bipolar number E-2 built by General Electric in 1919
- The only remaining Pennsylvania P5a, a 4-C-4 electric locomotive number 4700, the prototype, built by the Pennsylvania in 1931
- Union Pacific Big Boy number 4006, a 4-8-8-4 built by Alco in 1941
- Illinois Terminal number 1595, a (B-B)-(B-B) electric built in 1929 by the Illinois Traction for freight service
- New York Central number 113, a 2-D-2 electric built in 1906 by Alco-GE for service in Grand Central Terminal, New York
- One of the three GM Aerotrains, experimental articulated passenger trains built in 1955-56 by General Motors and tested on several railroads. Only one other survives.
- Duluth, Missabe & Northern number 502, a 1916 Baldwin 2-10-2 steam locomotive
- Chesapeake & Ohio number 2727, a 2-8-4 steam locomotive built by Alco in 1944
- Nickel Plate number 170, a 4-6-4 steam locomotive built in 1927 by Alco
- N&W number 2156, a class Y6a 2-8-8-2 steam locomotive built by the Norfolk & Western in 1942

And, of course, the museum holds a variety of interesting and unusual freight and passenger cars. Nonrevenue equipment in the collection includes a Union Pacific rotary snowplow (number 900081), an Illinois Central dynamometer car, and more.

And finally, fulfilling its role as a transportation museum, the Museum of Transportation has an automobile collection and collections of air and water transport artifacts. But it remains primarily a railroad museum, a really great one.

Orange Empire Railway Museum, Perris, CA

2201 A St
Perris, CA 92572
951-943-3020
www.oerm.org

Size	Rarity	Antiquity	Quality	Scope	Presentation
A	B	A	A	A	A

Land Area	90 Acres
Dates From	1956
Gauge	Mixed
Ownership	Private, Non-profit
Track	1 Mile
Locomotives	5 Steam 15 Diesel 6 Electric 1 Other
Rolling Stock	36 Passenger 70 Freight 16 Nonrevenue 65 Traction

The Orange Empire Railway Museum was founded in 1956 as a trolley museum. Initially located in Los Angeles' Griffith Park, the organizers leased the first piece of the land that now comprises the museum and moved onto in in 1958.

Interest in rail-

Pacific Electric car 418 was a 1913 product of Pullman. A "red car," also known as a "blimp," it saw service over several lines in the San Francisco Bay area and in Los Angeles before retirement in 1961.

roading beyond the world of the electric railways was present from the beginning, but got a major boost in the early 1990s when Ward Kimball (Disney's first and most important illustrator) donated most of his Grizzly Flats Railroad together with funds for its continuing operation and maintenance. With subsequent land purchases and the addition of many miles of track and wire, the museum is now one of the "really great" ones.

Today, although traction continues to predominate, the Orange Empire Railway Museum is a true railway museum with multiple gauges, steam, diesel and electric equipment all represented. With exceptions, the museum's scope is limited to the railroads of California and the southwest, but many interesting items are included. For example:

- Pacific Electric cars 1000 and 1001, gorgeous wood interurbans built by Jewett in 1913. Both have curved glass corner windows.
- Pacific Electric 150, an unusual trolley wire greaser built in 1898
- Los Angeles Railways' Descanso, a 1909 car designed especially for funeral service
- Atchison, Topeka & Santa Fe number 1999, a 24-stall horse-express car built in 1930 by Pullman
- Southern Pacific number 2445, an unusual articulated two-car coach set built by Pullman in 1941 for use on the SP "Daylights"
- Grizzly Flats number 2, an 1881 2-6-0 mogul built by Baldwin originally for the Nevada Central. It was Ward Kimball's primary steam locomotive.
- General American Transportation 705296, an unusual six-dome wine tank car built in 1941

The Great Museums

The great (but not really great) museums are the ones I would drive two hundred miles to visit. They, like the really great museums, are well worth multiple visits. The dedicated railfan should allow at least three hours just to walk through one of these museums and to see everything.

Seashore Trolley Museum, Kennebunkport, ME

195 Log Cabin Road
Kennebunkport, ME 04046
(207) 967-2712
www.trolleymuseum.org

Size	Rarity	Antiquity	Quality	Scope	Presentation
A	B	A	A+	A	A

Land Area	30 Acres
Dates From	1939
Gauge	Standard
Ownership	Private, Non-profit
Visit Suggestion	Morning
Track	1 Mile
Locomotives	1 Diesel
	8 Electric
Rolling Stock	1 Passenger
	15 Freight
	32 Nonrevenue
	173 Traction

The Seashore Trolley Museum is unabashedly an electric railroad museum and no pretense is made about it being anything else. But with the exception of this scope limitation, it is one of the great rail museums of the country featuring streetcar, rapid transit, interurban

Car 631 originally served on New York's Third Avenue Railway and is now at the Seashore Trolley Museum in Maine.

and electric freight equipment from all across the nation and, to a lesser extent, around the world.

Founded in 1939, the Seashore Trolley Museum is one of the oldest railroad museums in the world. Its first cars were stored and displayed on the land the museum now owns and, starting in 1953, the museum was able to operate its cars using electrical power from a motor-generator set donated by the New York Central. As traction lines were abandoned in the late 1940s and through the 1950s, Seashore Trolley Museum benefited from significant acquisitions and grew far beyond the founder's original hopes.

Today, the Seashore Museum's collection includes cars from the East (Maine to Virginia), the Midwest (Chicago, North Shore & Milwaukee and Cedar Rapids & Iowa City, for instance) and the West (Los Angeles and San Francisco). In addition, the museum collects, restores, displays and operates a fleet of historic buses including gas, diesel and trolley-bus variants.

In addition to more than a hundred-fifty streetcars, interurbans and rapid transit cars, the Seashore Trolley Museum holds a number of significant and interesting pieces including:
• Massachusetts Bay Transit Authority (MBTA) number 3424, a 1977 Boeing-Vertol light rail vehicle.

- Chicago, North Shore & Milwaukee number 415, an unusual interurban diner built by Cincinnati Car Company in 1926
- Cedar Rapids & Iowa City number 118, one of a group of very lightweight and highly powered cars built by Cincinnati Car Company in 1930. Fitted with a stainless steel 'cow-catcher," this car presents an impressive and usual frontal appearance.
- Lehigh Valley Transit number 1030 built by American Car and Foundry in 1931 in competitive response to the Cincinnati cars like CRANDIC 118. LVT 1030 is the only car saved from the Liberty Bell Route of Allentown, Pa.
- US DOT cars SOAC1 and SOAC2, experimental cars built by St. Louis Car Company in 1972 in hopes of duplicating the success of the 1935 President's Conference Committee car, the ubiquitous "PCC." (SOAC stands for "State Of the Art Car.")
- Portsmouth, Dover & York Street Railway number 108, a rare electric RPO built by Laconia Car Company in 1904
- Atlantic Shore Line Railway number 100, a steeple-cab type locomotive built by Laconia Car Company in 1906

And finally it should be noted that the Seashore Museum operates what could be the best gift shop in the world of railroad museums. The author finds it impossible to go into it and leave with his wallet intact.

Shore Line Trolley Museum, East Haven, CT

17 River St
East Haven, CT 06512
(203) 467-6927
www.bera.org

Size	Rarity	Antiquity	Quality	Scope	Presentation
B	A	A+	A	B	A

Land Area	5 Acres
Dates From	1945

Gauge	Standard
Ownership	Private, Non-profit
Visit Suggestion	Morning
Track	1 Mile
Locomotives	10 Electric
Rolling Stock	23 Nonrevenue
	82 Traction

When, in 1947, the Connecticut Company ceased service on the traction line that ran east from New Haven to Stony Creek, operations were immediately taken over by a group of enthusiasts who called themselves the Branford Electric Railway Association. A mile and a half of that line

One of the strengths of the Shore Line Trolley Museum is its collection of New York City subway cars. This is IND steel car number 1689.

remains in use today and is the basis of the Shore Line Trolley Museum. Shore Line, today, is a true trolley museum, concentrating exclusively on electric railroading.

One of the unusual aspects of the Shore Line Trolley Museum is its significant collection of New York City subway and elevated equipment. In addition to subway and elevated cars dating from 1878 through 1955, the museum holds a number of service cars that traveled the system in off-hours and were only rarely seen by the public. For instance:

- Interboro Rapid Transit number 95, a 1914 garbage collection hopper
- Manhattan Railway number 824, an elevated instruction car built in 1881
- Brooklyn Rapid Transit number 999, an elevated instruction car built in 1905
- Brooklyn Rapid Transit number 9832, a 1915 snow sweeper

- Interboro Rapid Transit car G, an elevated car built in 1878 and converted into a money collection car in 1893

Shore Line's collection goes well beyond the New York City rapid transit and totals well over a hundred pieces. Other items of special interest include:

- Montreal Tramways number 5 built in 1910, the only surviving electric rotary snow plow
- Interboro Rapid Transit number 3344, the Mineola, an unusual rapid transit parlor car
- The Derby, a steeple-cab electric locomotive built in 1888 by Pullman for the Derby Horse Railway. The Derby is believed to be the oldest electric locomotive in existence.
- Fourteen Canadian streetcars, interurbans and related pieces of equipment
- Cars from Iowa, Virginia, Washington DC, Georgia and even Austria

East Broad Top Railroad, Rockhill, PA

421 Meadow Street
Rockhill, PA 17249
(814) 447-3011
www.ebtrr.com

Size	Rarity	Antiquity	Quality	Scope	Presentation
B	C	C	A	C	A+

Land Area	16 Acres
Dates From	1873 (railroad) 1960 (museum)
Gauge	36 Inch
Ownership	Private For-profit/Non-profit
Visit Suggestion	Morning
Track	4 Miles
Locomotives	7 Steam 3 Diesel 2 Other (motorcars)

Rolling Stock	9 Passenger 53 Freight 1 Nonrevenue

The East Broad Top Railroad has long been operated through an agreement between the for-profit corporation that actually owns the equipment and land, and a volunteer non-profit organization that brings it all to life and runs trains. Regrettably the railroad is

East Broad Top number 15, a 2-8-2 Mikado, is shown entering the turntable after a run. The locomotive was built by Baldwin in 1914.

not operating and the museum is closed as this book is written, but it is included here in the hope that operations will resume and the museum will re-open soon.

The East Broad Top was originally a narrow-gauge coal-hauling railroad, first opened for business in 1873. When coal operations ceased in 1956, the railroad was sold for scrap, but the scrapper took no action and the entire railroad, intact, was left. Four years later, it reopened as a tourist operation and ran as such for more than fifty years.

In Rockhill, the visitor to the East Broad Top could see the company's offices and shops including a roundhouse, turntable, machine shop and other structures. He or she could also see several steam locomotives and often could watch them run and ride behind them. Because of its authenticity, the quality of maintenance and restoration, and the degree to which the railroad was complete and representative of early twentieth century railroading, the East Broad Top was, and hopefully will again be, a great museum.

The fascination of the East Broad Top revolves primarily around its completeness as an operating railroad and the total environment the visitor finds. But specifically of interest are:

- Six narrow-gauge steam locomotives, all Baldwin-built 2-8-2 Mikados and all dating from 1911 through 1923
- A coach and two combines, number 8, 14 and 15, built in 1882 by the Laconia Car Company and purchased by the East Broad Top from the Boston, Revere Beach & Lynn in 1916
- Number 20, the parlor car, built in 1882 by Billmeyer & Smalls and purchased by the East Broad Top from the Big Level and Kinzua in 1907.
- Several operable freight cars and long strings of inoperable coal hoppers that decorate the Rockhill yard.

Railroad Museum of Pennsylvania, Strasburg, PA

300 Gap Rd
Strasburg, PA 17579
(717) 687-8628
www.rrmuseumpa.org

Size	Rarity	Antiquity	Quality	Scope	Presentation
B	A	A	A+	B	A

Land Area	13 Acres
Dates From	1963
Gauge	Standard
Ownership	Public
Visit Suggestion	Morning
Locomotives	23 Steam 6 Diesel 6 Electric 6 Other
Rolling Stock	24 Passenger 27 Freight 6 Nonrevenue

The Railroad Museum of Pennsylvania would qualify for "really great" status except for its relative lack of diversity: it is more than half devoted to the history of the Pennsylvania Railroad and more than eighty percent to eastern railroading. For Pennsy fans it is the Mecca of

PRR number 5741 is a class G5s 4-6-0 designed primarily for suburban commuter service.

railroad museums but for others who simply enjoy seeing trains, it remains well worthwhile: great, but not "really great."

The Railroad Museum of Pennsylvania began with the historical collection of the Pennsylvania Railroad, which was originally assembled for the 1939-40 New York World's Fair. Following the merger of the Pennsylvania and the New York Central, the collection was endangered, but the Commonwealth of Pennsylvania stepped in. Ground was broken for the current museum in 1972; Penn Central first leased and then sold most of the collection to the state with the sale completed in 1979.

Items of special interest on display include:
- Pennsylvania Railroad E6s No. 460, the "Lindberg locomotive," a 4-4-2 Atlantic built in Juniata in 1914
- Pennsylvania Railroad K4s No. 3750, a 4-6-2 Pacific built in Juniata in 1920
- Pennsylvania Railroad M1b No. 6755, a 4-8-2 Mountain built in Juniata in 1930
- Pennsylvania Railroad Nos. 3936 and 3937, DD-1 electrics built in Juniata in 1911
- Pennsylvania Railroad No. 4800, the prototype GG-1 built by GE/Baldwin in 1934

- Amtrak No. 603, an E60 electric locomotive built by GE in 1976
- Camden & Amboy Railroad coach No. 3 built by the Camden & Amboy Shops circa 1836
- Pullman Company Lotos Club restaurant-sleeper built by Pullman in 1913
- Amtrak Metroliner number 860 built by Budd in 1968

Steamtown National Historic Site, Scranton, PA

4 Lackawanna Ave
Scranton, PA 18503
(570) 340-5200
www.nps.gov/stea

Size	Rarity	Antiquity	Quality	Scope	Presentation
A	C	B	A	B	A

Land Area	40 Acres
Dates From	1984
Gauge	Standard
Ownership	Public
Visit Suggestion	Afternoon
Track	1 Mile
Locomotives	28 Steam
	4 Diesel
Rolling Stock	37 Passenger
	28 Freight
	8 Nonrevenue

Steamtown began life as the private collection of F. Nelson Blount, an early railfan and collector. When Blount died in 1967, the collection gathered dust and rust for some years after being moved from Bellows Falls, Vermont to Scranton, Pennsylvania. Then, in 1988 following a highly-controversial authorization slipped through Congress late at night, the collection and the ex-Delaware, Lackawanna & Western yard in Scranton was taken over by the US Park Service. It is now a National Historic Site and the only railroad museum owned and operated by the federal government.

The Park Service subsequently utilized some existing track and spent $80 million to renovate the remaining portions of the 1902 roundhouse

Steamtown is home to this preserved Union Pacific Big Boy. The locomotive lives outdoors, but is kept in decent non-operating condition.

and shops and build additional facilities. Today the site is nearly unique in its urban setting, highly appropriate for the railroad and the era being celebrated.

Displayed in and around the buildings are more than eighty pieces of railroad equipment, notably including:

- Boston and Maine Railroad 3713, a 4-6-2 Pacific built by Lima in 1934
- Grand Trunk Western Railway 6039, a 4-8-2 Mountain built by Baldwin in 1925
- Meadow River Lumber Company 1, a two-truck Shay built by Lima in 1910
- New York, Chicago & St. Louis Railroad ("Nickel Plate Road") 759, a 2-8-4 Berkshire built by Lima in 1944
- The Reading Company 2124, a 4-8-4 Northern built by Baldwin in 1947
- Union Pacific Railroad 4012, a 4-8-8-4 Big Boy built by Alco in 1941
- Canadian National Railways 47, a 4-6-4T "Baltic tank" built by Montreal in 1914
- Canadian Pacific Railway 2317, a 4-6-2 pacific built by Montreal in 1923

Southeastern Railroad Museum, Duluth, GA

3595 Buford Hwy
Duluth, GA 30096
(770) 476-2013
www.srmduluth.org

Size	Rarity	Antiquity	Quality	Scope	Presentation
A	B	B	A	A	A

Land Area	35 Acres
Dates From	1956
Gauge	Standard
Ownership	Private, Non-profit
Visit Suggestion	Morning
Locomotives	9 Steam 8 Diesel 1 Other
Rolling Stock	28 Passenger 29 Freight 9 Nonrevenue 3 Traction

The Southeastern Railroad Museum does a great job of displaying its roster of equipment. Much of it is indoors, protected from the elements but, unlike other museums, the indoor display space is well lit and the tracks are separated by enough distance so the visitor can actually see and appreciate the rolling stock. Much of the passenger stock and even some of the freight cars have been restored inside and out and are open to the public, a nice touch that is beyond what some many museums are able to accomplish.

Now located in a suburb some twenty miles northeast of the center of Atlanta, the Southeastern Railroad Museum began in 1956 with an effort to save Atlanta & West Point number 290, a Lima-built heavy 4-6-2 Pacific. Display space was found in Atlanta's Lakewood Park where the annual Southeastern Fair was held. Space at Lakewood Park was soon filled to overflowing, but in 1965 the Southern Railway donated a twelve-acre plot east of Atlanta in Gwinnett County. The museum moved its growing collection, then consisting of some 34 cars and loco- motives, to that site starting in 1970.

This is how railroad antiques should be dis- played: indoors to protect them from the elements, well-lit, and with spacious aisles on both sides. Savannah & Atlanta number 750 lives at Duluth Georgia's Southeastern Railroad Museum.

The collection continued to grow and by the middle 1990s was approaching its current size and had filled the Gwinnett County location. Then, in 1997, thirty acres of land on the Norfolk Southern was donated and the museum moved to its present site. The move was greatly facilitated by the Norfolk Southern, which shut down its mainline for a day. Since that time, addi- tional plots of land have been purchased and a great deal of work has been done. The Southeastern Railroad Museum is now the official transportation museum of the State of Georgia by act of the legislature.

Among the notable pieces displayed are:
- Savannah & Atlanta number 750, a light 4-6-2 Pacific built in 1910 by Alco
- An H. P. Hood & Sons express milk reefer (GPEX 1015), par- tially restored but displayed with the doors open so the visi- tor can see the internal tanks.
- Campbell Limestone number 9, a 1923 Heisler
- Chattahoochee Valley number 21, a 2-8-0 consolidation
- Southern number 6901, an EMD E8 restored and appearing in Southern green and white
- NYO&W number 10, a GE 44-ton diesel

Mid-Continent Railway Museum, North Freedom, WI

E8948 Diamond Hill Rd.
North Freedom, WI 53951
(608) 522-4261
www.midcontinent.org

Size	Rarity	Antiquity	Quality	Scope	Presentation
B	C	A	A	B	B

Land Area	9 Acres
Dates From	1959
Gauge	Standard
Ownership	Private, Non-profit
Visit Suggestion	Mid-Day
Track	7 Miles
Locomotives	13 Steam
	5 Diesel
	2 Other
Rolling Stock	38 Passenger
	51 Freight
	14 Nonrevenue

Like many other museums, the Mid-Continent Railway Museum is located quite some distance from any large urban area and can be a chore to reach. Locations "far from urban areas," of course, are where land is cheap and where there are relatively few hassles about occasional clouds of coal smoke and occasional toots from an air horn. In the case of the Mid-Continent Museum, the effort to get to it is well worthwhile.

The Mid-Continent Railway Museum originated in 1959 as the Railway Historical Society of Milwaukee. Members put several items on display and wanted to run trains, but the owner of the rail line would not allow the use of steam. In 1963, when the Chicago & Northwestern abandoned a 4-mile branch in central southwestern Wisconsin near the town of North Freedom, the chapter bought it and has operated out of that location ever since.

The collection has grown significantly since 1959 and is now one of the dozen largest

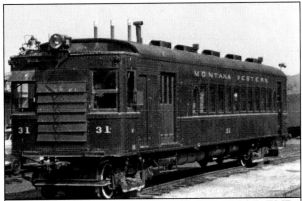

Montana Western number 31 is a 1925 EMD gas-electric car. It is the oldest surviving EMD gas-electric that remains in its original configuration.

in the country. Of particular note is the large collection (more than thirty) of pre-WWI passenger cars, many of them wood-sided and/or with wood underframes. The quality of restoration is high and the presentation of the completed work is good with one exception: the rarest and most valuable pieces are stored indoors, necessary to protect them from the weather. Unfortunately the storage building was designed with only narrow aisles between the tracks, the museum has seen fit to obstruct those aisles with stairways and platforms, and lighting in the building is inadequate.

Items of special interest and appeal at the Mid-Continent Railway Museum include:
• The collection of ancient passenger cars mentioned above
• Chicago & Northwestern boxcar number 10, a 36" gauge boxcar and one of the few pieces of Wisconsin narrow gauge still existing
• Wisconsin Fish Commission car, the Badger number 2, built for transport of fish from hatcheries to streams and rivers around the state. It contains fifteen tanks plus accommodations for crew
• A Milwaukee Road 1947 Dodge inspection car equipped to operate on the tracks.
• The museum's collection of thirteen steam locomotives, several of which are in the process of restoration.

The Mid-Continent Railway Museum gets high marks for communications with visitors. A hand-out brochure details the history and unique features of every item on display.

Lake Superior Railroad Museum, Duluth, MN

506 W Michigan St
Duluth, MN 55802
(218) 733-7519
www.lsrm.org

Size	Rarity	Antiquity	Quality	Scope	Presentation
B	A	A	A	B	B

Land Area	5 Acres
Dates From	1973
Gauge	Standard
Ownership	Private, non-profit
Visit Suggestion	Morning
Track	28 Miles
Locomotives	8 Steam
	16 Diesel
	2 Electric
	2 Other (RDCs)
Rolling Stock	24 Passenger
	28 Freight
	7 Nonrevenue
	1 Traction

The Lake Superior Railroad Museum is located under the train shed of historic Duluth Union Depot, which is both a good thing and a bad thing. It's good because the site itself is worth seeing and because the museum's collection is protected from the elements, which can be severe in Duluth. It's bad because the train shed is full and, relatively speaking, dark, making the collection hard to see, photograph and appreciate.

Duluth Union Depot was designed in the French Norman style by Peabody & Stearns of Boston. It opened in 1892 and over the years served the Duluth, Missabe & Iron Range, Great Northern, Northern Pacific, St. Paul & Duluth and Duluth, South Shore & Atlantic.

Milwaukee Road 10200 and DM&IR 227 are posed together at the Lake Superior Transportation Museum.

The depot was built with six stub tracks and a seventh through track. At one point there were fifty arrivals and fifty departures daily under a massive train shed. The train shed was replaced with individual platform canopies in 1924 and in 1969 passenger service came to an end.

In 1971 Duluth Union Depot was purchased from the railroad with the idea of turning it into a museum center and it is now owned by St. Louis County. The Lake Superior Railroad Museum was founded in 1973 and with the help of the railroads, began to collect rolling stock and fill the tracks. While the 1924 butterfly canopies are still in place, a new roof has been added over them, enclosing much of the collection and protecting both it and visitors from the weather. In the middle 1980s a parking lot was erected over the tracks south of the new roof and it provides protection for still more equipment.

What sets the Lake Superior Railroad Museum apart from other museums and what makes it "great," is the quality of its collection, the rarity of several locomotives, and the high state of their preservation. In Duluth one can see:

- Milwaukee Road electric number 10200, the only remaining one of its class, built by General Electric in 1915
- DM&IR Yellowstone number 227, a 2-8-8-4 steam locomotive built by Baldwin in 1941
- The William Crooks, a 4-4-0 American class, the Great Northern's first steam locomotive, built in 1861 by Smith

and Jackson of the New Jersey Locomotive and Machine
Company of Paterson, NJ.

- The Minnetonka, Northern Pacific's first locomotive, an 0-4-0
  built in 1870 by Smith and Porter of Pittsburgh
- A McGiffert Self-Propelling Log Loader, built by the Clyde
  Iron Works in Duluth in 1923
- United States Steel Duluth Works slag car No. 6, built in
  1915

Colorado Railroad Museum, Golden, CO

17155 W 44th Ave
Golden, CO 80403
303-279-4591
www.coloradorailroadmuseum.org

Size	Rarity	Antiquity	Quality	Scope	Presentation
B	A	A+	A	B	A

Land Area	15 Acres
Dates From	1959
Gauge	Mixed
Ownership	Private, Non-profit
Visit Suggestion	Mid-Day
Locomotives	15 Steam 5 Diesel 3 Other
Rolling Stock	32 Passenger 62 Freight 10 Nonrevenue

The Colorado Railroad Museum is known for its large collection
of western narrow gauge and especially for the three Denver &
Rio Grande Southern "galloping geese" it holds and displays.
But there's more: standard gauge steam and diesel are also
represented in significant numbers. There's a roundhouse with
a very rare dual-gauge turntable and one can see the relocated

stainless steel model vista-dome car that was originally placed in Glenwood Canyon in 1950 to mark the spot where the vista-dome concept was first imagined.

Denver & Rio Grande number 683 stands outside the Richardson library.

The museum was originally the private collection of Bob Richardson, who moved to Colorado in 1948 and began buying old equipment. Richardson's collection was soon supplemented with items saved and donated by others, especially including Cornelius Hauck, who is now considered to be co-founder of the modern museum. When Richardson's storage space filled up in 1959, the collection was moved to the existing site in the city of Golden and in 1965 the Colorado Railroad Historical Foundation was formed to take over the museum.

Interesting pieces in the collection include:
- A long list of steam including Denver & Rio Grande Western 683, an 1890 Baldwin 2-8-0, and 318, another Baldwin 2-8-0 but from 1896; Colorado Central 40, a 1920 Baldwin 2-6-0; Chicago, Burlington & Quincy 5629 a 4-8-4 Northern built in 1940 by the railroad; Denver, Leadville & Gunnison number 191 a 2-8-0 from Baldwin in 1880; Denver & Rio Grande Western number 491, a 2-8-2 from Baldwin in 1902
- Diesels including Coors number 988, a 1957 EMD SW8; Rio Grande 5771, an EMD F9A diesel and 5762, its sister B-unit.
- Manitou & Pikes Peak number 1, an 0-4-2T cog-wheel locomotive from Baldwin in 1893
- Argentine Central number 14 and West Side Lumber number 12, both Lima shays
- Denver & Rio Grande Western geese number 2, 6 and 7
- Standard and narrow gauge passenger and freight cars including the Navajo, an Atchison, Topeka & Santa Fe Super

41

Chief round-end, rib-side observation car and Denver & Rio Grande Western number 60, a narrow-gauge RPO
- Colorado & Southern steam rotary snowplow number 99201
- Two cars by Billmeyer & Small, four by Jackson & Sharp, two by Barney & Smith and even a very rare car by the Wagner Palace Car Company. These early carbuilders are poorly represented in museums today because they have been so long out of business.

Cumbres & Toltec Scenic Railroad, Chama, NM

500 Terrace Ave   5234 B US Hwy 285
Chama, NM 87520   Antonito, CO 81120
719-376-5483
www.cumbrestoltec.com

Size	Rarity	Antiquity	Quality	Scope	Presentation
A	B	C	A	C	A

Land Area	48 Acres
Dates From	1880 (railroad); 1971 (museum)
Gauge	36 Inch
Ownership	Public/Private, Non-profit
Visit Suggestion	Afternoon
Track	64 Miles
Locomotives	10 Steam 1 Diesel 1 Other
Rolling Stock	45 Passenger 120 Freight 39 Nonrevenue

The important attraction at the Cumbres & Toltec is the ride between Chama and Antonito, an incredible sixty-three miles each way, but there is also a lot to see just walking through its unfenced yard including steam locomotives, freight and passenger cars and work equipment, essentially all of it original to the railroad. There are also massive wooden water and coaling towers, two narrow-gauge rotary plows (the OM and the OY) and much more.

In 1967 the Denver & Rio Grande Western abandoned the last major segment of its narrow-gauge operations in

Cumbres & Toltec 2-8-2 number 488 slumbers outside the Chama engine house on a day off.

southern Colorado, striking a significant blow to the economy of the area. Together, the states of Colorado and New Mexico purchased the scenic portion between Antonito, Colorado and Chama, New Mexico and hired professional firms to operate the line starting in 1971. The arrangement was successful until, at the end of the 1999 season, contract disputes arose that led to the firing of the current operating firm. No satisfactory bids were received from other operators so, rather than see the line shut down, the previously-nonprofit Friends of the Cumbres & Toltec submitted an ultimately successful bid and operated the line for five years. After that, operations were taken over by other firms but, as of this writing, the bi-state commission that controls the railroad is looking at options for the 2013 season.

The Cumbres & Toltec yard at Chama contains the largest collection of narrow gauge equipment in the country. While there's a balloon track and an engine and car shop in Antonito, the main shops, the storage yard and most of the equipment is in Chama when it is not in use on the road. And, best of all, the Chama yard is open to those who would carefully wander through it. It's quite easy to spend two hours, just wandering.

In addition to the coaling and water towers and the 1899 depot, look especially for the ten 2-8-2 Mikados, five of them class K36, four class K37 and a single class K27. Also worth seeing are the two rotary snowplows OM and OY, spreader OU, and the three flangers: OJ, OK and OL.

Nevada Northern Railway Museum, Ely, NV

1100 Avenue A East
Ely, NV 89301
866-407-8326
nevadanorthernrailway.net

Size	Rarity	Antiquity	Quality	Scope	Presentation
A	C	A	A	C	A

Land Area	21 Acres
Dates From	1906 (railroad); 1986 (museum)
Gauge	Standard
Ownership	Public
Visit Suggestion	Morning
Track	8 Miles
Locomotives	4 Steam 10 Diesel 2 Electric
Rolling Stock	11 Passenger 69 Freight 13 Nonrevenue

The Nevada Northern Railway, an outgrowth of the Eureka & Palisade, opened for business in 1906, primarily to carry copper ore and concentrate from the Nevada Consolidated Copper mine west of Ely to the smelter in McGill, Nevada, a distance of twenty miles.

Over the decades, mining activity declined and trucks became more efficient than the railroad. Passenger service ended in 1941 and the last ore was moved by rail in 1978, although a small amount of local freight continued to be handled. Kennecott Copper (the corporate successor to Nevada Consolidated Copper) donated most of the railroad to the White Pine Historical Society and tourist operations began in 1986.

Today the Nevada Northern ranks high among railroad museums partly because of its size and the amount of equipment available to be seen and experienced, but also because it is, in

Steam locomotives 40 and 93 in the Nevada Northern engine house. Number 40 is a 1910 Baldwin 4-6-0 and 93 is a 1909 Alco 2-8-0. Both were built for the Nevada Northern and have been on the property for more than a hundred years.

itself, a complete railroad, almost unchanged from the years just before World War II. Only the East Broad Top of Rockhill, Pennsylvania and the Cumbres & Toltec of Chama, New Mexico compare in this regard.

Primary items of interest at the Nevada Northern include:
- Three steam locomotives original to the railroad: Number 40, a 1910 Baldwin 4-6-0; number 81, a 1917 Baldwin 2-8-0; and number 93 a 1909 Alco 2-8-0
- Two electric locomotives (80 and 81), both GE, one 75-ton, the other 85-ton, used by the railroad in McGill, Nevada to switch the smelter
- An Alco RS-2 and an RS-3, a Baldwin VO-1000, and a Baldwin-Lima-Hamilton S-12 diesel, all original to the railroad, plus other diesels, some acquired in later years.
- Nevada Northern number "A", a hundred-ton steam-powered wrecking crane built by Industrial Works of Bay City, MI in 1907
- Nevada Northern number "B", an Alco-Cooke 1907 steam-powered rotary snow plow
- The original East Ely depot and freight shed; the original engine house and car house (tours are available)

- A large and open yard where careful and responsible railfans are allowed to wander essentially at will
- A large concrete coaling tower and steel water tower. Both are now out of service, but retain their original appearance.

California State Railroad Museum, Sacramento, CA

125 "I" Street
Sacramento, CA 95814
(916) 445-7387
www.csrmf.org

Size	Rarity	Antiquity	Quality	Scope	Presentation
B	A+	A	A	B	A

Land Area	2 Acres
Dates From	1981
Gauge	Mixed
Ownership	Public
Visit Suggestion	Mid-Day
Track	3 Miles
Locomotives	19 Steam
	19 Diesel
	1 Electric
	1 Other
Rolling Stock	21 Passenger
	30 Freight
	8 Nonrevenue

The California State Railroad Museum is a formal museum. Everything is protected from the elements and the visitors. Equipment is beautifully restored to non-operating condition and nicely displayed. Unfortunately only a percentage of the museum's collection can be displayed and the remainder is stored off-site, invisible to the visitor. The museum does occasionally admit researchers to its off-site storage and a tour may be possible with an advance request. At least it won't hurt to ask.

First opened in 1981, the existing museum is administered by the California Department of Parks and Recreation. It sits on a rail line originally built by the Sacramento Southern, within yards of buildings that rec-

The Southern Pacific built cab-forward steam locomotives to protect its crews from smoke and poisonous gasses in the long Sierra mountain tunnels. This is the only one still in existence.

reate the Central Pacific's Sacramento freight and passenger stations, and just across the tracks from the huge complex that was once the Southern Pacific shops. Politics, finances, the state's economy, and the museum's relationship with various railroad managements have resulted in development plans that have come and gone over the years, but the site has incredible history and extensive potential. A still greater museum is very likely in the future.

The California State Railroad Museum's collection is understandably about eighty-five percent Western railroading. While both narrow gauge and standard gauge equipment is well represented, electric railroading is almost ignored. These scope limitations, while not lessening the value of the collection, do keep the museum out of the "really great" list.

The most notable equipment at the California State Railroad Museum includes:
- Southern Pacific number 4294, a class AC-12 4-8-8-2 cab-forward by Baldwin in 1944
- The Gold Coast, an 1895 wood framed private car that once belonged to Lucius Beebe
- The Governor Stanford, an 1862 Norris 4-4-0, the first of the Central Pacific's locomotives

- The Genoa, Virginia & Truckee's locomotive number 12, an 1873 Baldwin 4-4-0
- The Sonoma, the North Pacific Coast Railroad's number 12, an 1876 Baldwin 4-4-0
- The C P Huntington, first locomotive on the Southern Pacific, built by Danforth & cook in 1863, a rare 4-2-4T
- Nevada Short Line number 1, a 36" gauge 2-6-0 built by Baldwin in 1879

And in addition to this list, the museum displays several later steam and diesel locomotives and a variety of both standard and narrow gauge freight and passenger cars, including several from the nineteenth-century and others from the twentieth.

Although it has only indirect connection to the railroads, it's also worth noting that the California State Railroad Museum hosts a large and colorful collection of fruit crate labels from the early years of the twentieth century. They're appropriately displayed inside a 1924 wood-sided FGE ice reefer.

But my favorite of all the displays at the California State Railway Museum is a 1929 Canadian Pacific Pullman sleeper with a hidden mechanism that gently rocks it as though it were moving down the track. The sleeper's windows are blacked out and another machine furthers the simulation of the train's motion by making occasional crossings lights and bells roll past outside the darkened windows. It's a perfect evocation of a night journey by Pullman. I'd pay a pretty sum to be allowed to spend the night there.

Western Pacific Railroad Museum, Portola, CA

700 Western Pacific Way
Portola, CA 96122
(530) 832-4131
www.wplives.org

Size	Rarity	Antiquity	Quality	Scope	Presentation
A	C	C	B+	C	B

Land Area	36 Acres
Dates From	1984
Gauge	Standard
Ownership	Private, Non-profit
Visit Suggestion	Morning
Track	1 Mile
Locomotives	1 Steam 36 Diesel 1 Electric
Rolling Stock	18 Passenger 86 Freight 12 Nonrevenue

The Western Pacific Railroad Museum is unabashedly devoted to the history and the rolling stock of a single railroad: the Western Pacific. It is quite large at thirty-six acres of land and about a hundred-fifty items of on-rail equipment, but falls short of "really great" status in the areas of antiquity and scope.

Western Pacific 805-A was originally built as part of a three unit A-B-A set for the California Zephyr. Although it is shown with an F9B rather than the original F7B, the impact is there.

Started by the Feather River Rail Society, the museum was sparked by the 1983 donation of F7 locomotive 921 to the City of Portola, California. The Society leased the recently vacated Portola diesel shop, brought together other privately-owned and donated items, and the Portola Railroad Museum was underway. Today the society boasts more than a thousand members and the renamed museum, a huge collection.

Almost two-thirds of the equipment in the Western Pacific Railroad Museum is post-war, with diesel engines and freight cars predominating. Despite the museum's name and its avowed focus on the Western Pacific, almost half of the equipment comes from other western railroads and a few items come from the Midwest. Highlights include:

- Kennecott Copper number 778, a 125-ton electric built by General Electric in 1958. It is believed to be the last steeple-cab locomotive ever built.
- Western Pacific 165, a 1919 Alco 0-6-0 switcher
- Union Pacific Centennial diesel number 6946
- Western Pacific numbers 805A and 925C, EMD FP7A and F9B units, respectively. Both were built in 1950, 805A specifically for California Zephyr service.
- Four lightweight Budd passenger cars from the California Zephyr: two dome chair cars, a dome lounge and a diner (Silver Lodge, Silver Rifle, Silver Hostel and Silver Plate).
- An unusually large collection of sixteen cabooses of almost all kinds
- Simplot/JRSX number 5021, an unusual cryogenic reefer built by Pacific Car and Foundry in 1968
- A huge collection of diesel locomotives with virtually all the significant manufacturers represented.

The Really Good Museums

The "really good" museums are the ones that are too good to be called just "good." Without exception, they house and display equipment that is rare, interesting and well worth seeing and I wouldn't pass within a hundred miles of any of them without trying very hard to find time for a visit. Allow at least two hours of your time to see these museums and more than that if you plan to take a ride or stop to study any particular piece in detail.

Connecticut Trolley Museum, East Windsor, CT

58 North Road
East Windsor, CT 06088
(860) 627 6540
www.ct-trolley.org

Size	Rarity	Antiquity	Quality	Scope	Presentation
B	B	A	B	B	B

Land Area	17 Acres
Dates From	1940
Gauge	Standard
Ownership	Private, Non-profit
Track	2 Miles
Locomotives	2 Diesel
	6 Electric
	1 Other
Rolling Stock	3 Passenger
	14 Freight
	6 Nonrevenue
	41 Traction

The Connecticut Trolley Museum operates on a 17-acre plot that includes a portion of the Rockville branch of what was once the Hartford & Springfield Street Railway Company. The land was

51

purchased and the museum founded in 1940 and since that time, volunteers have been laying track and stringing wire to accommodate the museum's growing collection.

As its name implies, the Connecticut Trolley Museum is an electric railroading museum and is one of the few museums

This partly-restored Baldwin-Westinghouse freight motor was built in 1918 as number 18 for the Oshawa Railways of Oshawa, Ontario in Canada.

in this book that does not own a steam locomotive. But there's still lots to see and a number of truly rare and unusual pieces.

The collection includes:

- Montreal Tramways number 4, an open-top tourist car with tiered seating
- Ponemah Mills 1386, an 1894 General Electric steeple-cab electric freight locomotive
- Singer Company 132 and 143, two boxcars built in 1869 for the sewing machine company
- Four Chicago elevated cars (numbers 4175, 4284, 4409 and 4436) with build dates from 1914 to 1951.
- Durbin & Greenbrier Valley Railroad number LEV 2, a 1980 Leyland diesel-hydraulic passenger car with a bus body. It looks like a bus, but isn't.
- Canadian National number 6714, a heavy-duty mainline electric locomotive built in 1917 by General Electric for passenger service on the Canadian Northern through Montreal's Mount Royal tunnel.

Danbury Railway Museum, Danbury, CT

120 White St
Danbury, CT 06813
203-778-8337
www.danbury.org/drm

Size	Rarity	Antiquity	Quality	Scope	Presentation
B	C	B	B	C	B+

Land Area	**19 Acres**
Dates From	**1994**
Gauge	**Standard**
Ownership	**Private, Non-profit**
Visit Suggestion	**Afternoon**
Locomotives	**1 Steam**
	13 Diesel
	3 Other
Rolling Stock	**16 Passenger**
	24 Freight
	7 Nonrevenue

When Metro-North closed Danbury Union Station, the 1903 Colonial Revival building was taken over by a group of railroad enthusiasts and renamed the Danbury Railway Museum. After extensive renovation, the building reopened in 1994.

New York, New Haven & Hartford RS-1 number 673 smokes up a storm at the Danbury Railway Museum as all good Alcos should.

Danbury Union Station is located on a balloon track at the end of what was originally the New Haven's Danbury Branch. Directly across the tracks – and inside the loop – the New Haven built a holding yard and a small locomotive service facility. The roundhouse is long gone, but the yard and the turntable remain, both under the museum's control and both used to display its collection; the station is where the organization's tourist trains depart.

The Danbury Railroad Museum's collection is sizeable given the short twenty years the organization has been in operation. There is a strong emphasis on standard gauge northeast railroading with only a few Canadian pieces originating outside New York and New England. But there are also some remarkable things to be seen:

- Canadian National FPA-4 number 6786 joined by FPB-4 number 6867. These are Alco-designed units looking much like the well-known FA, but equipped for passenger service, built by the Montreal Locomotive Works, and currently painted (as of this writing) as New York Central 1930 and 3399. In particular, the FPB-4, a cab-less "B" unit, is extremely rare.
- Metro-North number GCT-1, an unusual double-ended 100-ton wrecking crane designed for use in the Grand Central Terminal tunnels. It is powered from the third rail.
- Remington Arms number 2, a 1954 railbus built by the Mack Truck Company. Intended for short-line passenger use, it was sold to Remington instead, then passed to Sperry Rail Service and finally to the museum. Ten were built, one other survives in Spain.

Pennsylvania Trolley Museum, Washington, PA

1 Museum Road
Washington, PA 15301
(724) 228-9256
www.pa-trolley.org

Size	Rarity	Antiquity	Quality	Scope	Presentation
C	C	B	A	C	A

Land Area	14 Acres
Dates From	1963
Gauge	Mixed (Standard/Broad)
Ownership	Private, Non-profit
Visit Suggestion	Mid-Day
Track	1 Mile
Locomotives	3 Diesel
	5 Electric
Rolling Stock	2 Freight
	9 Nonrevenue
	35 Traction

A group of Pittsburgh electric railfans bought a small single-truck Pittsburgh trolley in 1949. In 1953 Pittsburgh Railways abandoned its line from Pittsburgh to Washington, PA and the group was able to buy a half-mile of right-of-way. That line, with subse-

Philadelphia and West Chester Traction Car 78 waits to pick up passengers.

quent additions, forms the basis of today's museum. What was originally known as the Arden Trolley Museum opened its doors to the public in 1963.

Hurricane Ivan brought flooding and significant damage in 2004, but repairs have been finished and a new display building was opened in 2005. The new building is well-lit and spacious, allowing most of the collection to be stored under cover while providing access and visibility for visitors.

Interestingly, the museum includes a number of pieces of broad-gauge (62.5") equipment. That gauge was (and still is) common in Philadelphia.

Several pieces at the Pennsylvania Trolley Museum are of particular interest:
- Federal St. & Pleasant Valley Railway car number 101, an 1885 horsecar
- Toledo Railways "Toledo," an unusual 1906 Brill private street railway car
- Boston Elevated Railway 3618 and Pittsburgh Railway M551, both 1920s self-propelled side-dump electric hoppers by the Differential Car Company
- West Penn Railways number 1, a tiny home-built electric locomotive from 1915
- Armco Steel number B73, a 1930 Baldwin/Westinghouse 68-ton "visibility cab" diesel with a most unusual and striking external appearance.

Strasburg Rail Road, Strasburg, PA

300 Gap Rd
Strasburg, PA 17579
717-687-7522
www.strasburgrailroad.com

Size	Rarity	Antiquity	Quality	Scope	Presentation
B	C	A	A	C	B

Land Area	14 Acres
Dates From	1837 (railroad); 1958 (museum)
Gauge	Standard
Ownership	Private, For-profit
Visit Suggestion	Morning
Track	4 Miles
Locomotives	9 Steam
	2 Diesel
	3 Other
Rolling Stock	28 Passenger
	15 Freight
	4 Nonrevenue

The Strasburg Rail Road was chartered by the Commonwealth of Pennsylvania in 1832 and began operation in 1837. As the nearby Pennsylvania Railroad was built, the Strasburg became a feeder line, running from Strasburg to a connection at Leaman Place, just east of Para-

Strasburg 475 is a 4-8-0 twelve-wheeler built by Baldwin in 1906 for the Norfolk & Western.

dise, PA and three and a half miles away. When the railroad filed for abandonment, a group of railfans stepped in and bought all of the company's stock. Today, Strasburg, with the exception of the Baltimore & Ohio, is the oldest continuously-operated railroad in the country.

The Strasburg promotes itself almost exclusively as a train ride. But it is also a museum with a number of interesting locomotives and cars available for viewing in the yard. Notably, the Strasburg also operates one of the country's leading contract steam locomotive restoration shops, so visiting power can often be seen.

At Strasburg, you might look for:
- The railroad's remarkable collection of twenty-eight passenger cars. What's remarkable about them is the fact that (with the exception of three Canadian National baggage cars), the newest was built in 1913 and the oldest in 1896.
- Reading number 87, an 0-4-0 camelback. The 87 was undergoing restoration as this was written and may not be available to the visitor
- Grasse River railcar number 10, built in 1915 by the Sanders Machine Shop
- Pennsylvania 7002, a 1902 4-4-2 Atlantic type. Originally number 8063, the locomotive was renumbered by the PRR to stand in for the record-setting 7002 at the 1939 New York World's Fair. The original 7002 was (unreliably) clocked at 127 miles-per-hour in 1905. It may not have actually gone that fast, but still it was a very fast locomotive. (The 7002 actually belongs to the Pennsylvania Historical and Museum Commission; it is listed on the Strasburg roster, but could move across the street to the Railroad Museum of Pennsylvania at any time.)

North Carolina Transportation Museum, Spencer, NC

411 South Salisbury Ave
Spencer, NC 28159
(704) 636-2889
www.nctrans.org

Size	Rarity	Antiquity	Quality	Scope	Presentation
A	A	C	A	B	A

Land Area	57 Acres
Dates From	1983
Gauge	Standard
Ownership	Public/Private, Non-profit
Track	2 Miles
Locomotives	8 Steam 12 Diesel 1 Electric 1 Other
Rolling Stock	30 Passenger 40 Freight 13 Nonrevenue 2 Traction

The North Carolina Transportation Museum is one of the largest railroad museums in the country in terms of land area. Located in what used to be the Southern Railroad's Spencer shops, it includes the railroad's giant backshop building, its full half-circle original round-

This unusual and obviously experimental auto rack is at the North Carolina Transportation Museum.

house and turntable, and a number of other original buildings. Plan on walking a significant distance if you want to see everything.

The Southern Railroad closed its steam locomotive repair facilities in 1960 but continued to operate the classification yard in Spencer for almost another twenty years. The first portion of the land that now makes up the museum was donated to the State of North Carolina in 1977 with other donations following. A non-profit support group was also created in 1977 and the museum first opened to the public in 1983. An eight million dollar restoration was completed in 1996 but work continues.

Restoration standards are high and most of the equipment on site appears complete. Items on display include:

- Atlantic Coast Line number 501 painted in ACL purple, a 1939 EMD E3
- Seaboard Air Line steam locomotive 544, a 2-10-0 Decapod built by Alco in 1918
- Duke Power number 111, an 0-4-0T saddle-tanker built by Alco circa 1922
- Piedmont & Northern number 5103, a boxcab electric built by General Electric in 1913. Number 5103 is unusual in that it carries both a trolley pole and a pantograph
- Southern Railways E8 number 6900 painted in Southern green and white, an EMD product of 1951
- Graham County Railroad 3-truck Lima Shay number 1925 built in 1925
- Atlantic Coast Line 1031, a 1913 Baldwin 4-6-0
- Norfolk Southern number 1616, a Baldwin-Lima-Hamilton AS-416 diesel built in 1955
- Southern Railway 542, a 2-8-0 consolidation built by Baldwin in 1903
- Beaufort and Morehead number 1860, a Fairbanks-Morse H-12-44 built in 1950
- Southern Railways 2601, an EMD GP30 of 1963
- Southern Railways number 6133, an EMD FP-7 of 1950 in Southern green and white
- The Hampton & Branchville Railroad M-200 motor car built in 1926 by the Edwards Railway Motor Car Company
- Southern number 599000, a three-unit articulated auto rack
- Three private cars including the *Loretto,* built for Charles Schwab, the *Carolina*, a railroad business car, and the *Doris*, built for James Duke.
- Southern number 49, a fully restored RPO displayed with the interior open to visitors
- US Army 89480, a restored Army hospital car, complete with restored interior and displayed with the interior open to visitors

Gold Coast Railroad Museum, Miami, FL

12750 SW 152 St
Miami, FL 33177
(888) 608-7246
gcrm.org

Size	Rarity	Antiquity	Quality	Scope	Presentation
B	B	C	B	B	A

Land Area	34 Acres
Dates From	1957
Gauge	Standard
Ownership	Private, Non-profit
Visit Suggestion	Afternoon
Locomotives	2 Steam
	7 Diesel
Rolling Stock	19 Passenger
	13 Freight
	3 Nonrevenue

The Gold Coast Railroad Museum had its start in 1957 when a donated steam locomotive (Florida East Coast number 153) was moved onto an ex-Naval base then used by the University of Miami. The collection was given a major boost in 1959 when the ex-presidential rail car *Ferdinand Magellan* arrived. In 1966 the museum was forced to move and ended

Seaboard Air Lines number 6300, a tavern/lounge car, was built by Budd in 1939 for the New York-to-Florida Silver Meteor. After serving Amtrak and a list of private owners, it arrived at the Gold Coast museum in 2003.

up in Fort Lauderdale, but moved back to its present location in Dade County in 1983. The *Ferdinand Magellan* was named a

National Historic Landmark in 1985 and, partly as a result, the museum's collection grew dramatically. Then, in 1992, hurricane Andrew hit, causing major damage. With assistance from FEMA and many donors, that damage has now been repaired and the museum's buildings strengthened for the future.

The Gold Coast Railroad Museum has a number of interesting pieces on display, but two stand out:

- The F*erdinand Magellan,* a heavyweight passenger car, was built by Pullman in 1927 and modified in 1942 specifically for use by the President. In addition to an elegant interior, it is armor-plated and has both bullet-proof glass and steel doors. At 285,000 pounds, the *Ferdinand Magellan* is the heaviest passenger car ever used in the USA.
- MHAX 1202, a very unusual helium transportation car. It carries pressurized helium (at 3000 psi) in a series of individual tanks mounted lengthwise on the car's floor.

Heart of Dixie Railroad Museum, Calera, AL

1919 9th St
Calera, AL 35040
(205) 668-3435
www.hodrrm.org

Size	Rarity	Antiquity	Quality	Scope	Presentation
B	B	C	B	A	A

Land Area	13 Acres
Dates From	1963
Gauge	Standard
Ownership	Private, Non-profit
Visit Suggestion	Morning
Track	5 Miles
Locomotives	4 Steam
	11 Diesel
	2 Electric

Rolling Stock	27 Passenger
	21 Freight
	12 Nonrevenue

The Heart of Dixie Railroad Museum originated in Birmingham, Alabama, initially storing and displaying its equipment on the Louisville & Nashville Railroad across the tracks from the Alabama Power steam generation plant and close to today's Amtrak station. Vandalism in the

One of several "critters" (small industrial locomotives) at the Heart of Dixie Railroad Museum. This one is Alabama Dry Dock & Shipbuilding Company's number 520-020. It is a 52-tonner, built by General Electric in 1942.

unfenced area became a problem, however, and in 1983 the club moved, purchasing land in the small town of Calera, a little more than thirty miles south of Birmingham.

The land in Calera was adjacent to the Alabama Mineral Railroad, a one-time Louisville & Nashville subsidiary that had been abandoned by the L&N when a new hydroelectric dam flooded trackage and submerged an important bridge site. Along with the land, the museum was able to purchase eleven miles of right-of-way, five of which have now been restored and are used for the museum's demonstration trains.

While the museum's collection contains almost no nineteenth-century equipment, there are still some interesting and unusual pieces:
- Empire Coke numbers 1 and 2, a pair of small, four-wheel electric steeplecabs. Their maker and date are unknown but they're no later than the 1920s and could be from before World War I.
- Alabama Power Co number 40, a 1953 Davenport 0-4-0 fireless steam locomotive

63

- Woodward Iron Co number 38, a 2-8-0, a 1928 Baldwin coal-burner
- Alabama Byproducts number 4046, a 1948 Lima 0-6-0
- Long Island Rail Road commuter coach number 2972, a 1956 product of Pullman, a long way from home.
- Louisville & Nashville 42476, a fully restored wood-bodied camp car originally built as a boxcar in 1921. While camp cars are common in museums, their restoration is unusual.
- Amtrak numbers MRLX 1400 and 1403, material handling cars built by Thrall in 1986. These cars were part of a mid-1980s effort by Amtrak to capture mail and express business and while they aren't old, they are unusual in museums.

In addition to these pieces, the Heart of Dixie Railroad Museum displays a significant amount of unrestored freight equipment and a string of light- and heavyweight passenger cars. A number of "critters," small diesel or gas locomotives of uncertain design and heritage are also interesting.

In addition to the on-rail equipment, there is a nice display of railroad signals. The museum also owns and operates an extensive two-foot gauge park railroad that features a propane-powered steam locomotive originally built for the Birmingham Zoo.

An active CSX track (ex-L&N) runs close to the property, making a nice railfanning opportunity.

Kentucky Railroad Museum, New Haven, KY

136 S Main St
New Haven, KY 40051
800-272-0152
www.kyrail.org

Size	Rarity	Antiquity	Quality	Scope	Presentation
B	C	C	B	C	B

Land Area	12 Acres
Dates From	1954
Gauge	Standard
Ownership	Private, Non-profit
Visit Suggestion	Mid-Day
Track	17 Miles
Locomotives	5 Steam
	10 Diesel
	1 Other
Rolling Stock	24 Passenger
	32 Freight
	11 Nonrevenue

The Kentucky Railroad Museum is located in the small town of New Haven, Kentucky, almost fifty miles south of the center of Louisville. Like many railroad museums, it went through several rented and temporary locations before it grew to the point where it could purchase property and achieve perma-

US Army 1846, a 1953 H12-44 Fairbanks-Morse diesel at the Kentucky Railroad Museum.

nence. What is now the museum's site was originally a Louisville & Nashville branch between Boston and Mount Vernon, Kentucky. The museum owns seventeen miles of track in addition to the museum and workshop property.

The most remarkable piece in the collection is Chesapeake & Ohio 2-8-4 Kanawha number 2716, which is stored under cover in presentable non-operating condition. Other steam includes Louisville & Nashville number 152, a 1905 light pacific by Rogers that is normally kept in operating condition. Number 152 is the oldest Pacific-type held by any of the museums in this book and most likely the oldest in the United States. Interesting diesels include Chicago, Indianapolis & Louisville Railway (Monon) number 32, an EMD BL2 unit, Louisville & Nashville 770, an EMD E6A (without its prime mover, but possibly the only E6 in existence) and Atchison, Topeka & Santa Fe 2546, a CF7. And finally, the museum has almost seventy pieces of passenger, freight and non-revenue rolling stock.

Indiana Transportation Museum, Noblesville, IN

825 Park Drive
Noblesville, IN 46060
(317) 773-6000
www.itm.org

Size	Rarity	Antiquity	Quality	Scope	Presentation
B	A	B	B	A+	B

Land Area	6 Acres
Dates From	1960
Gauge	Standard
Ownership	Private, Non-profit
Visit Suggestion	Morning
Track	4 Miles
Locomotives	2 Steam
	10 Diesel
	4 Electric
Rolling Stock	39 Passenger
	37 Freight
	11 Nonrevenue
	16 Traction

The Indiana Transportation Museum was formed in 1960, unrelated to the Indiana Railway Museum described on page 118. With a small but growing collection, the organization obtained land in Forest City Park in Noblesville, Indiana near the center of the state and moved onto it, opening there in 1968.

In subsequent years, the museum has prospered and has developed several innovative programs, notably including a partnership with the Indiana State Fair through which the museum uses its equipment to ferry fairgoers from a northern suburb of Indianapolis

Twin Branch number 4 was designed primarily for battery operation. The small pantograph on the roof was used for charging the battery.

onto the fairgrounds. Success, however, has meant an increasing collection and the museum's space is now close to full. A little more than half the rostered equipment is stored and inaccessible to the casual visitor.

Equipment of note at the Indiana Transportation Museum includes:

- Singer number 1, a tiny electric locomotive that spent its life switching cars at the Singer Sewing Machine plant in South Bend. It is notable for being the second oldest preserved electric locomotive in the country (the oldest being the Derby, which is at the Shore Line Trolley Museum in Connecticut).
- Twin Branch number 4, a heavy duty Baldwin/Westinghouse battery-powered locomotive. Locomotives that used batteries as primary power sources were rare and very few have been saved.
- Florida East Coast number 90, an 1898 product of Jackson & Sharp; Henry Flagler's second private car. The original incredible interior is essentially intact.

National Railroad Museum, Green Bay, WI

2285 South Broadway
Green Bay, WI 54304
(920) 437-7623
www.nationalrrmuseum.org

Size	Rarity	Antiquity	Quality	Scope	Presentation
B	C	B	B+	A	B+

Land Area	**33 Acres**
Dates From	**1956**
Gauge	**Standard**
Ownership	**Private, Non-profit**
Visit Suggestion	**Mid-Day**
Track	**1 Mile**
Locomotives	**11 Steam** **11 Diesel** **1 Electric** **1 Other**
Rolling Stock	**18 Passenger** **19 Freight** **4 Nonrevenue**

Despite its modest size compared to some other railroad museums, the National Railroad Museum really is the national railroad museum; a 1958 joint resolution of Congress made it so. Unfortunately the resolution didn't include funding, so today the National Railroad Museum, like many others,

This 1956 GM Aerotrain is one of only three ever built. It was sleek and stylish according to the thinking of the times, but was also underpowered, hard to maintain, hard-riding and uncomfortable.

lives entirely on donations, admissions and gift shop and ticket sales.

The National Railroad Museum is comprised of a loop of track, three major buildings, several smaller buildings and outdoor display tracks. One building houses the visitor center along with an area used for temporary displays and a large and interesting collection of passenger train tail signs. The second building contains four tracks and five concrete walkways. Unfortunately it is not well lit and the walkways are narrow.

However, the third building, where the museum's premier exhibits are displayed, is a model of how these things should be done. It contains five tracks, but the outside aisles have been eliminated, the tracks spread apart and excellent lighting provided.

Items of special interest at the National Railroad Museum include:
- One of two surviving GM Aerotrains including the locomotive and two cars
- The British locomotive number 60008 the *Dwight D Eisenhower*, a 4-6-2 Pacific, and two British passenger cars
- Union Pacific 4-8-8-4 Big Boy number 4017
- Pennsylvania Railroad GG-1 number 4890
- Richter Vinegar Co car number 20, a wood-tank vinegar car
- TTX flat car 970837 with a Schneider semi-trailer loaded on it. While this car isn't especially old, it is interesting to see the details of how the trailer is attached.

Minnesota Transportation Museum, St. Paul, MN

193 Pennsylvania Ave E
St Paul, MN 55130
651-228-0263
www.trainride.org

Size	Rarity	Antiquity	Quality	Scope	Presentation
B	C	B	B	B	B

Land Area	9 Acres
Dates From	1962
Gauge	Standard
Ownership	Private, Non-profit
Visit Suggestion	Morning
Track	5 Miles
Locomotives	3 Steam 10 Diesel 2 Other
Rolling Stock	28 Passenger 28 Freight 3 Nonrevenue

The Minnesota Transportation Museum operates the Osceola & St. Croix Valley Railway of Osceola, WI (a train ride), the Minnehaha Depot in Minneapolis, MN, and the Jackson Street Roundhouse, a museum in St. Paul. It is the roundhouse that concerns us here.

Northern Pacific caboose 1264 was built by the railroad in 1901. Nicely restored, it sits in front of the Jackson Street Roundhouse.

When the St. Paul & Pacific Railroad was first built, it began at St. Paul, Minnesota, the headwaters of navigation on the Mississippi River, and ran north along the river. Land was set aside for a steam locomotive servicing facility on the north side of the city close to the Jackson Street crossing. After receivership and a name change, the railroad came under the control of James J Hill and in 1890 it was merged with the Montana Central, the Minneapolis & St Cloud and other railroads to form the Great Northern. In 1907 the Great Northern built the roundhouse and shops complex that exists today. Dieselization was completed in 1957 and the Jackson Street roundhouse was closed in the late

1960s. It served for a time as a warehouse but then became the home of the Minnesota Transportation Museum.

Among the Minnesota Transportation Museum's more interesting and unusual pieces are:

- Dan Patch Lines number 100. This locomotive was built as a very early gas-electric in 1913. In 1918 its engine was removed and it was converted to run as an electric under overhead wires. In 1957 a diesel engine was added and number 100 was taken off the overhead, serving until its retirement in the early 1960s.
- Armco number B71, a Westinghouse "visibility cab" switcher. As a transition unit between the earliest box-cab diesels and the more streamlined, later units, the B71 presents an unusual and interesting outline and also represents an uncommon manufacturer.
- Great Northern number 400, the Hustle Muscle, built in 1966, the first 3600 horsepower turbo-charged 20 cylinder 645E3 production model SD45 by EMD.

Monticello Railway Museum, Monticello, IL

992 Iron Horse Pl
Monticello, IL 61856
(217) 762-9011
www.mrym.org

Size	Rarity	Antiquity	Quality	Scope	Presentation
B	C	B	B	A	B

Land Area	20 Acres
Dates From	1966
Gauge	Standard
Ownership	Private, Non-profit
Track	2 Miles
Locomotives	4 Steam 10 Diesel

Rolling Stock	26 Passenger 35 Freight 16 Nonrevenue

The Monticello Railway Museum had its beginning in 1966 as an organization dedicated to encouraging steam excursions on the CB&Q. Having little success, it began a program of equipment collection, initially to operate its own trips, but when land became

Colorful Canadian National FPA-4 number 6789 is at the Monticello Railway Museum.

available in Monticello, Illinois, the transition to a museum (with operations) was begun. Today the museum has a twenty-acre yard, several buildings, and twelve miles of ex-Illinois Central and ex-Illinois Terminal right-of-way.

Among the interesting items held by the Monticello Railway Museum are:
- Southern Railway number 9838, a slug built in 1977 from an Alco RS-3 chassis built in the early 1950s
- CB&Q 14042, an 1892 caboose still riding on wood beam trucks
- The Nautilus, once the J. G. Shedd Aquarium's fish transport car
- Wabash 1189, a 1953 F7a built by GMD (of Canada), painted in Wabash colors and operational

Nevada State Railroad Museum, Carson City and Boulder City, NV

2180 S Carson St
Carson City, NV 89701
(775) 687-6953
www.nsrm-friends.org

600 Yucca Street
Boulder City, NV 89005
(702) 486-5933

Size	Rarity	Antiquity	Quality	Scope	Presentation
A	A+	A+	A	C	B

Land Area	57 Acres
Dates From	1980
Gauge	Mixed
Ownership	Public
Track	4 Miles
Locomotives	11 Steam
	6 Diesel
	8 Other
Rolling Stock	37 Passenger
	39 Freight
	10 Nonrevenue

The Nevada State Railroad Museum is narrowly focused on the railroads of the region. The museum's collection is divided between two locations, Carson City and Boulder City. Both are well worth a visit.

Virginia & Truckee number 25, a Baldwin 4-6-0, dates from 1905 and is kept in operating condition by the Nevada State Railroad Museum.

The State of Nevada got its first historic steam locomotive in 1943 with the donation of the Carson & Tahoe Lumber & Fluming Company's *Glenbrook* by a private party. But it wasn't until the nostalgia wave of the 1960s that serious efforts were made to collect and display equipment. Much was obtained from the film industry that had originally been bought and restored as movie props; more came from elsewhere in the entertainment industry.

The State Legislature gave responsibility for the collection to the Nevada State Park System in 1973 and in 1980 the Carson City museum was opened. Since the Carson City site lacked space for anything more than token operation of the restored equipment, a site was selected and added to the museum in Boulder City at the end of the ex-Union Pacific branch line to Boulder Dam. While there is equipment to see at Boulder City, the site is primarily dedicated to the seven-mile round trip ride.

As a state-owned and state-funded organization, restoration is meticulous, but access is limited, almost entirely to fully-restored equipment. In Carson City, two items are of special interest:

- The Inyo, an 1875 Baldwin 0-4-0 built for the Virginia & Truckee. It is in operable condition and is operated on occasion.
- Virginia & Truckee number 22, a McKeen motorcar. Number 22 is the only surviving McKeen car in operating condition.

Also of interest in Carson City:

- Carson & Tahoe Lumber & Fluming number 1, the Glenbrook, an 1875 Baldwin 2-6-0
- Dayton, Sutro & Carson Valley number 1, the Joe Douglass, an 1882 Porter 0-4-2T
- Virginia & Truckee number 18, the Dayton, a 4-4-0 built by the Central Pacific in 1873
- Tucson, Cornelia & Gila Bend number 401, a 1926 Edwards motorcar
- A collection of fourteen Virginia & Truckee standard gauge passenger cars built between 1868 and 1907. This collection includes the coach that was once Charles Crocker's private car
- Virginia & Truckee number 1005, a twenty-eight foot long boxcar, now fully restored

The collection at Boulder City includes both steam and diesel locomotives and more.

- Of key interest is a four-piece narrow gauge collection that includes three ancient passenger cars from the Eureka & Palisade and the Eureka-Nevada plus an 1896 2-8-0 steam locomotive from Utah's Uintah Railway. Unfortunately all are unrestored and off-limits to the casual visitor.
- Union Pacific GP30 number 844 in Union Pacific paint and with its rooftop ductwork intact. It is one of very few preserved GP30s.

Pacific Southwest Railroad Museum, Campo, CA

Hwy 94 and Forrest Gate Road
Campo, CA 91906
(619) 478-9937
www.sdrm.org

Size	Rarity	Antiquity	Quality	Scope	Presentation
B	C	B	B	A	A

Land Area	21 Acres
Dates From	1961
Gauge	Standard
Ownership	Private, Non-profit
Visit Suggestion	Mid-Day
Track	5 Miles
Locomotives	6 Steam
	17 Diesel
	1 Other
Rolling Stock	25 Passenger
	37 Freight
	2 Nonrevenue

The Pacific Southwest Railroad Museum operates two facilities, one, a historic depot, in downtown La Mesa, California, the other, another depot some forty miles southeast in the city of Campo. The La Mesa location is small and very urban, while the much larger Campo facility is where almost all of the museum's equipment is stored and displayed.

The classic Pullman heavyweight lounge/observation car: The *Robert Peary* was built in 1927 for private rental and reportedly saw use by President Franklin Roosevelt, opera star Lily Pons and screen stars Nelson Eddy and Jeanette MacDonald.

Founded in 1961, the museum began running trains on unused rail spurs in the San Diego metropolitan area and on Naval Air Station Miramar in the late 1960s. In 1980 land adjacent to the mainline of the San Diego & Arizona Eastern Railway was purchased in the city of Campo and all equipment was moved there. Since then, the Campo site has grown to include a fifteen track museum yard, a three stall engine house, shops and a display building.

There's some really interesting stuff to see at the Pacific Southwest Railroad Museum. For instance:

- California Western number 46, a 2-6-6-2 articulated logging engine built by Baldwin in 1937
- San Diego & Arizona number 1809 and USA number 1820, both MRS-1 (Military Road Switcher) units from EMD built in 1952 during the Korean War with gauge-adjustable trucks to allow operation in a variety of locations. The museum also has USAF number 2104, the Alco version of the MRS-1.
- San Diego & Arizona coach number 239, a wood car by the very unusual builder, Gilbert & Bush. At this writing, the museum holds only the car body.
- Rockdale, Sandow, & Southern Railroad number 3, a Jim Crow combine with a racial segregation divider in the coach section. Number 3 has been fully restored.

- Santa Maria Valley Railroad number 9, a tiny railbus built by Fairmont in 1932. Riding on just four wheels and powered with a Ford model A engine, it carried mail and express north of Los Angeles until 1936.

Western Railway Museum, Suisun City, CA

5848 State Highway 12
Suisun City, CA 94585
(707) 374-2978
www.wrm.org

Size	Rarity	Antiquity	Quality	Scope	Presentation
B	A	B	A	C	A

Land Area	22 Acres
Dates From	1946
Gauge	Standard
Ownership	Private, Non-profit
Visit Suggestion	Morning
Track	6 Miles
Locomotives	2 Steam
	3 Diesel
	10 Electric
Rolling Stock	7 Passenger
	15 Freight
	8 Nonrevenue
	45 Traction

The Western Railway Museum is almost exclusively an electric railroad museum focusing on the streetcar and interurban lines of the west coast. Begun, as are almost all railroad museums, with the acquisition of a single car, by 1960 space was needed and a site in Rio Vista Junction on the historic Sacramento Northern was acquired. Since then, the museum has grown significantly. A new visitor center and a new four-track display barn join several other shop and restoration buildings and twenty-two miles of track originally built by the Oakland, Antioch, and Eastern Railway.

The museum holds several interesting and unique pieces:

Four cars line up in front of the main barn at the Western Railroad Museum

- Sacramento Northern number 1, a portable substation car. These cars were heavily cannibalized for parts when taken out of service, so very few of them remain. Sacramento Northern 1 has been mechanically restored and is actually used to power the museum's wires when trains are run.

- A train of three Key System "bridge cars," (numbers 182, 186 and 187) built to run over the San Francisco-Oakland Bay Bridge. The cars have a unique appearance with deep skirting and large windows.

- Richmond Shipyard Railway 561 and 563 are ex-New York City elevated cars built in 1887 and electrified when the elevated line steam engines retired. They may be the only surviving equipment from the steam elevated lines.

- Blackpool Transit number 226 is an odd-looking "boat car," built in 1934 to haul people to and from the British seaside resort. It is an open car with swept-up ends resembling a boat's prow.

- San Francisco Municipal Railway 1258, a Boeing–Vertol Light Rail Vehicle was built in 1974, retired in 2002 and is of special interest primarily because it is so recent.

- Salt Lake & Utah number 751 is an open-platform observation car that was originally convertible and could operate either as a coach or a parlor car. Now painted an eye-catching red, the car serves in the museum's demonstration rides.

Railtown 1897 State Historic Park, Jamestown, CA

AKA Sierra Railroad
5th Ave and Reservoir Rd
Jamestown, CA 95327
(209) 984-3953
www.railtown1897.org

Size	Rarity	Antiquity	Quality	Scope	Presentation
B	A	A	B+	C	A

Land Area	8 Acres
Dates From	1897 (railroad); 1992 (museum)
Gauge	Standard
Ownership	Public
Visit Suggestion	Afternoon
Track	6 Miles
Locomotives	5 Steam
	6 Diesel
	3 Other
Rolling Stock	19 Passenger
	32 Freight
	10 Nonrevenue

The Sierra Railroad, originally a logging and mining line, achieved fame and survival by becoming a site where many movies have been made over the years. Since 1992 it has survived, mostly intact, as the property of the State of California and an arm of the California

The view inside the Sierra roundhouse hasn't changed in a hundred years. This photo was taken in 2012.

State Railroad Museum. In addition to being open to the public, The Sierra Railroad still occasionally gets involved in the film business.

The Sierra Railroad's roundhouse, turntable, and shops are the setting. The "stars" of the show are several ancient but still operable steam locomotives and a variety of period passenger and freight equipment. Highlights of the collection include:

- Steam locomotives 3, 28 and 34. Number 3 is an 1891 Rogers 4-6-0, while numbers 28 and 34 are Baldwin 2-8-0s, number 28 having been built in 1922 and number 34 in 1925.
- Two three-truck Lima Shays, number 2 dating from 1922 and number 7 from 1925
- Central Pacific number 43, an ancient open platform coach by the Wason Manufacturing Company dating from 1869
- A Southern Pacific tea-and-silk car of unknown make dating from circa 1903 (this car consists of the body only)
- A California Dispatch Line wine tank car by Pullman dating from 1911
- A 1905 Yosemite Short Line box car originally built to run on 30-inch gauge track.

Sumpter Valley Railroad, Baker City, OR

Austin St
Sumpter, OR 97877
(541) 894-2268
www.svry.com

Size	Rarity	Antiquity	Quality	Scope	Presentation
B	C	B	B	B	A

Land Area	22 Acres
Dates From	1976
Gauge	36 Inch
Ownership	Private, Non-profit

Visit Suggestion	Mid-Day
Track	5 Miles
Locomotives	3 Steam
	3 Diesel
	3 Other
Rolling Stock	3 Passenger
	40 Freight
	10 Nonrevenue

The original narrow-gauge Sumpter Valley Railroad was a logging line that ran west from Baker City, Oregon. As the timber was cut, the railroad extended itself, ultimately reaching as far as Prairie City, some sixty miles from Baker City. Mostly abandoned in

Locomotives 19 and 8 are steamed up and ready to go on the Sumpter Valley Railroad. Number 19 is a 2-8-2 Mikado built in 1920 for the Sumpter Valley; number 8 is a Heisler from the W. H. Eccles Lumber Company

1947, all operations had ceased and all rails and equipment were removed by 1961. Beginning in 1971, a group of enthusiasts began collecting equipment and making plans. With help from several local industries and, notably, from the Union Pacific, they have succeeded in re-establishing over five miles of track and, remarkably, have found and recovered a significant amount of the original equipment.

Today the Sumpter Valley Railroad operates between Sumpter, Oregon and a place in the middle of the valley known as McEwan. In Sumpter there is a restored depot and museum, but the rail equipment is stored and serviced in McEwan, where it can be seen by visitors. The stars of the show, of course, are the railroad's three steam locomotives: a 1915 Heisler and two 1920 Alco 2-8-2 Mikados. The Heisler came from the W.H. Eccles Lumber Co. via Boise Cascade, but the two Mikados were originally Sumpter Valley locomotives. They were retrieved from the

White Pass and Yukon, where they had lived as numbers 80 and 81 since 1940.

Other than the steam locomotives, possibly the most distinctive aspect of the Sumpter Valley roster is the large amount of freight equipment on hand compared to passengers cars. Almost all of it was purchased from the East Broad Top, the White Pass & Yukon, and the Denver & Rio Grande (Western).

Northwest Railway Museum, Snoqualmie, WA

38625 SE King St
Snoqualmie, WA 98065
(425) 888-3030
www.trainmuseum.org

Size	Rarity	Antiquity	Quality	Scope	Presentation
C	B	B	B	C	B

Land Area	5 Acres
Dates From	1957
Gauge	Standard
Ownership	Private, Non-profit
Visit Suggestion	Morning
Track	3 Miles
Locomotives	9 Steam
	7 Diesel
	2 Other
Rolling Stock	15 Passenger
	34 Freight
	12 Nonrevenue

A trip to see the Northwest Railway Museum begins at the old Seattle, Lake Shore and Eastern Railway (later, Northern Pacific) depot in downtown Snoqualmie where the tourist trains board and where part of the museum's collection is displayed. Another part of the collection is stored on tracks that begin a block north and extend for the better part of a mile, and the balance is displayed under roof at the museum's exhibit building, a mile to the south (and accessible only by rail). This dispersion of the equipment is, in a sense, the cost of operating out of a historic downtown depot where space is severely limited.

Kennecott Copper number 201 is an Alco RSD4 from 1951. Operational, it is used to pull tourist trains at the museum.

A few items of special interest on the museum's roster:
- US Plywood number 11, a 2-6-6-2 compound mallet, originally Ostrander Railway and Timber number 7, It is one of the smallest standard-gauge mallets ever built
- Weyerhaeuser number 108, another 2-6-6-2 from Baldwin in 1926 (number 108 is a tank locomotive, so is really a 2-6-6-2T)
- And if two 2-6-6-2 locomotives aren't enough, the museum also has Weyerhaeuser number 6, a 1928 Baldwin 2-6-6-2
- Six other steam locomotives notably including Northern Pacific number 924, am 1899 0-6-0 from Rodgers Locomotive Works. Few Rodgers locomotives remain in collections today.
- Northern Pacific number 83296, a 1930 wood-bodied slat-sided stock car by Ryan Car Company, one of very few surviving stock cars from a rare builder
- Six log disconnects, three are from 1905, one from 1912 and two from 1916
- Kennecott Copper number 201 (pictured above), the only surviving RSD-4

The Good Museums

The creation of a railroad museum is a lot of work. One has to be concerned with land, track, building codes, occupancy permits, taxes or tax exemptions, complaining neighbors, environmental and safety issues, equipment purchases, repair and restoration work, federal and state regulation, staff, visitor amenities, security, insurance and, above all, money. Big railroad museums are fascinating, but smaller ones can be worth a visit too, especially those that evince decades of dedicated work by scores of volunteers.

We list below museums that don't qualify as great, but do have at least modest size and, often, something on display that is rare and interesting. They will all be worth a visit if you're nearby.

Conway Scenic Railroad, North Conway, NH

38 Norcross Circle
North Conway, NH 03860
603-356-5251
www.conwayscenic.com

Size	Rarity	Antiquity	Quality	Scope	Presentation
C	C	C	B	C	B

Land Area	7 Acres
Dates From	1974
Gauge	Standard
Ownership	Private, For-profit
Visit Suggestion	Mid-Day
Track	21 Miles
Locomotives	2 Steam
	7 Diesel
	1 Other

Rolling Stock	20 Passenger
	16 Freight
	4 Nonrevenue

The Conway Scenic Railroad is based in and its yards are adjacent to the original 1874 Portsmouth, Great Falls & Conway Railroad's North Conway station. That station, which features metal-roofed towers at each end in an exu-

Boston & Maine F7A number 4266 is a 1949 product of EMD.

berant display of Victorian architecture in the Russian provincial style, is highly evocative of its era and is actually one of the important draws. The history-minded railfan might visit the museum just to see the station.

The Conway Scenic Railroad is a tourist line, but is also a museum with significant amounts of equipment on display. The roster is almost exclusively twentieth-century, with three quarters of the pieces dating from after World War I and half from after World War II. There is a roundhouse and turntable. There are two F-units, two first-generation General Electric diesels, several geeps and a New York, New Haven and Hartford RDC. Passenger equipment includes a Norfolk & Western Powhatan Arrow diner; freight includes a Bangor & Aroostook mechanical reefer.

Maine Narrow Gauge Railway and Museum, Portland, ME

58 Fore Street
Portland, ME 04101
207-828-0814
www.mngrr.org

Size	Rarity	Antiquity	Quality	Scope	Presentation
C	A+	B	B	C	B

Land Area	**2 Acres**
Dates From	**1991**
Gauge	**24 inch**
Ownership	**Private, Non-profit**
Visit Suggestion	**Morning**
Track	**1 Mile**
Locomotives	**4 Steam**
	5 Diesel
	3 Other
Rolling Stock	**18 Passenger**
	12 Freight
	3 Nonrevenue

The Maine Narrow Gauge Railway and Museum is small by the standards of this book and might not be included except for the fact that it is the most important single repository of Maine two-foot gauge equipment.

Monson Railroad number 4, a 1918 Vulcan Forney 0-4-4T, poses under steam with two friends.

Following the abandonment of the Maine two-foot gauge railroads in the 1930s, Ellis Atwood purchased a significant amount of equipment and set it up on his cranberry farm in Massachusetts. Atwood's Edaville Railroad quickly became the Mecca of the two-foot lines, the place to go to see and experience the equipment. When Atwood died in 1950, his railroad continued to be operated by a succession of other managers, but it finally closed and equipment was sold in 1991, much of it ultimately going to the Maine Narrow Gauge Railway and Museum.

Today, four locations in Maine are recreating the miniature world of the tiny narrow gauge trains. The Maine Narrow Gauge Railway and Museum is the largest of the three, but the Waterville, Wiscasset & Farmington (Alna, ME), the Boothbay Railroad Village (Boothbay, ME) and the Sandy River and Rangeley Lakes (Phillips, ME) also have pieces and operate trains.

The two-foot gauge lines were never large and over the years their locomotives and rolling stock have become dispersed to a degree that makes it hard for the railfan to see much – except here. The Maine Narrow Gauge Railway and Museum has four steam locomotives, a Reo-based railbus, a Model T inspection car, six passenger cars, a snow plow and a flanger, all built for 24-inch gauge track. The Rangeley is the only 24-inch parlor car ever built. The museum is worth a visit.

New York Museum of Transportation, Rush, NY
Rochester & Genesee Valley Railroad Museum, West Henrietta, NY

6393 East River Road
West Henrietta, NY 14586
(585) 533-1113
www.nymtmuseum.org
rgvrrm.org

Size	Rarity	Antiquity	Quality	Scope	Presentation
C	C	C	C	C	B

Land Area	5 Acres
Dates From	1971
Gauge	Standard
Ownership	Private, Non-profit
Visit Suggestion	NYMT: Morning R&GV: Afternoon
Track	2 Miles
Locomotives	3 Steam 9 Diesel 4 Other
Rolling Stock	14 Passenger 15 Freight 9 Nonrevenue 11 Traction

The New York Museum of Transportation is located only a mile or two from the Rochester & Genesee Railroad Museum and the museums work closely together. Admission is on a single ticket and, interestingly, transportation between them is provided via a rail link that is half electric and half internal combus-

Lehigh Valley 211, an Alco RS3, was originally Pennsylvania 8445. It is unusual, being equipped with a steam generator and dynamic brakes.

tion – the visitor transfers between a streetcar and either a diesel-hauled train or a gasoline speeder in mid-trip.

The New York Museum of Transportation was formed in the early 1970s to provide a home for Rochester-area trolleys that had become available with the closure of a museum in Pennsylvania. Through the late 1970's, rail and ties were salvaged from the former Rochester Subway, additional cars were obtained, and the museum broadened its scope, adding a collection of highway vehicles. Electrification of the line was completed in 1996, allowing operation of the cars for the first time.

The Rochester & Genesee Valley was founded in 1971 when the Rochester Chapter of the National Railroad Historical Society purchased the Erie Railroad's Industry, NY depot from the Erie-Lackawanna Railroad. Volunteers restored the depot to its 1930's appearance and built a three-track yard to display restored railroad equipment. In 1995 the two-mile railroad that joins the museum to the New York Museum of Transportation was completed and transportation between the museums started the following year.

Considering both museums, there are collections of traction, diesel and three small steam engines, one of which is an unusual Heisler rod engine. There are a number of passenger cars (including a seven-car set of matched stainless steel cars from the New York Central's Expire State Express), a few freight cars and several restored cabooses. The museum houses a very early and rare 1920 Plymouth model BL gas-mechanical locomotive. The streetcar collection concentrates in large part on local city lines in the upstate New York region. Possibly the most interesting single piece of electric equipment is trolley sweeper C-130, ex of the Philadelphia streetcar system.

Lake Shore Railway Museum, North East, PA

31 Wall Street
North East, PA 16428
(814) 725-1911
www.grape-track.org

Size	Rarity	Antiquity	Quality	Scope	Presentation
C	B	C	C	A	B

Land Area	3 Acres
Dates From	1956
Gauge	Standard
Ownership	Private, Non-profit
Visit Suggestion	Mid-Day
Locomotives	1 Steam
	4 Diesel
	1 Electric
	2 Other
Rolling Stock	13 Passenger
	11 Freight

Some museums have appeal that transcends their size and the absolute rarity of the equipment on display. The Lake Shore Railway Historical Society runs such a place in the unlikely town of North East, Pennsylvania. North East is a small town and the museum is small, but the dedication of the volunteers is evident and the museum's location immediately on the ex-New

This 136-ton locomotive was built by General Electric for Ford in 1940 with styling that mimics a 1938 Ford automobile. In this photo, taken in 2009, the locomotive remains in need of work, but at least it has been saved from the scrappers.

York Central mainline to Chicago – still a very heavily used route – makes it a marvelous place to watch the trains go by.

Of special note, the Lake Shore Railway Museum has the only survivor of eight locomotives custom made in 1940 for Henry Ford's plant with sheet metal designed to resemble a 1938 Ford. It also has the only surviving boxcar from the Lake Shore & Michigan Southern Railroad, a 36-foot wood-framed car undergoing restoration, and it has an 1895 Barney & Smith business car, also built for the Lake Shore & Michigan Southern, and the last known LS&MS passenger car.

The Lake Shore Railway Museum has a Chicago, South Shore & South Bend Little Joe (a 2+D+D+2 heavy electric) and a 1910 electric car shunt built by the Atlas Car Company that saw service with Hewlett ship unloaders in Cleveland.

Railroader's Memorial Museum, Altoona, PA

1300 Ninth Ave
Altoona, PA 16602
(814) 946-0834
www.railroadcity.com

Size	Rarity	Antiquity	Quality	Scope	Presentation
C	C	C	B	C	B+

Land Area	11 Acres
Dates From	1965
Gauge	Standard
Ownership	Private, Non-profit
Visit Suggestion	Morning
Locomotives	2 Steam 1 Diesel 1 Electric 1 Other
Rolling Stock	10 Passenger 9 Freight 3 Nonrevenue

The centerpiece of the Railroader's Memorial Museum is Pennsylvania Railroad class K4s number 1361, a 4-6-2 Pacific and an example of one of the most successful steam locomotive designs of all time. Number 1361 spent twenty-eight years on display at Horseshoe Curve before being moved into Altoona for restoration and possible operation. That restoration remains in progress and, unfortunately, mired in political and financial battles between various groups, but we hope they will be resolved eventually and the locomotive will someday run again.

Pennsylvania Railroad GG-1 number 4913 appears in the Tuscan Red paint scheme first applied in January 1952. Only ten of the hundred thirty-eight GG-1s ever received red paint.

The Railroader's Memorial Museum is located in a portion of what was once the Pennsylvania Railroad's Altoona Shops, the largest rail shop complex in the world and home to as many as fifteen thousand workers. When Strasburg was selected as the site for the Railroad Museum of Pennsylvania (page 30) disappointed Altoona railfans organized and started work on their own museum. It took a long time, but ground was broken in 1979 and the Railroader's Memorial Museum opened in 1980.

The collection at the Railroader's Memorial Museum is almost entirely centered on the Pennsylvania Railroad and its corporate successors: Penn Central and Conrail. And, interestingly, at least half the equipment was built by the railroad and some was built in the shops complex now used to display it. Of interest is Pennsylvania 470245, a 1952 sixteen-axle, 250-ton depressed center flatcar that was known as the *Queen Mary* by railroad employees. Although flatcars are as common as oxygen at most railroad museums (because they're so useful), very few heavy-duty cars have been saved.

Rockhill Trolley Museum, Rockhill, PA

Meadow Street
Rockhill Furnace, PA 17249
(814) 447-9576
www.rockhilltrolley.org

Size	Rarity	Antiquity	Quality	Scope	Presentation
C	C	C	B	C	C

Land Area	3 Acres
Dates From	1962
Gauge	Standard
Ownership	Private, Non-profit
Visit Suggestion	Morning
Track	2 Miles
Locomotives	1 Diesel
	1 Electric
	1 Other
Rolling Stock	2 Freight
	9 Nonrevenue
	16 Traction

Founded in 1962, the Rockhill Trolley Museum was first known as the Shade Gap Electric Railway because it operated then and still operates now on the Shade Gap branch of the East Broad Top Railroad (page 28). Being literally within walking distance of each other, the two museums share

Car number 172 at the Rockhill Trolley Museum came from Oporto, Portugal. A single-truck Brill car, it features dynamic brakes, which are unusual in streetcars.

some dual-gauge track, but the Rockhill Trolley Museum is primarily standard gauge.

While the collection at the Rockhill Trolley Museum isn't over-whelming like some of the larger museums, it still does contain a number of items of real interest:

- York Railways 163 is a rare curved-side Brill car, the only one surviving. Cincinnati Car Company held the curved-side patent and sued Brill after this car and four others were built, ending curved-side construction at Brill.
- Philadelphia & Western number 205 was built by Brill in 1931. A modern mostly aluminum Brill "Bullet," 205 was originally designed for third-rail power collection. It now sports a trolley pole and is believed to be the only operating bullet anywhere.
- Philadelphia Subway number 1009 is a rapid transit car, designed for operation over the Ben Franklin Bridge and through the Broad Street Subway. A 1936 product of Brill, it has been restored to its original and striking blue and silver paint scheme.
- Red Arrow Lines *Independence Hall* is a four-car permanent-ly coupled train, originally built in 1941 for the Chicago, North Shore & Milwaukee. When that line ended service in 1963, *Independence Hall* and its sister, *Valley Forge*, were sold to the Red Arrow Lines where they operated until 1981. Independence Hall is powered by motors totaling a thousand horsepower and is capable of speeds well over ninety miles an hour.

Reading Railroad Heritage Museum, Hamburg, PA

500 South 3rd Street
Hamburg, PA 19526
(610) 562-5513
www.readingrailroad.org

Size	Rarity	Antiquity	Quality	Scope	Presentation
C	C	C	B	C	B

Land Area	2 Acres
Dates From	1976
Gauge	Standard
Ownership	Private, Non-profit
Visit Suggestion	Afternoon
Locomotives	14 Diesel 3 Other (2 RDCs)
Rolling Stock	25 Passenger 42 Freight 6 Nonrevenue

The Reading Company Technical and Historical Society was founded in 1976, initially as a repository for memorabilia and archival company records. The collection soon came to include locomotives and rolling stock, which were stored in the Reading Company

Reading number 5308 is an Alco C630, fully restored and in service.

shops building in Reading, PA until the loss of a lease in 1988 forced a move of the small artifacts to a museum building in Hamburg and the on-rail equipment to a yard in Leesport. Since that date, essentially everything has been consolidated on the property in Hamburg.

As might be expected, three-quarters of the museum's collection consists of equipment that at one time bore Reading Company reporting marks. The collection is actually quite large, at least given the relatively small size of the railroad: about fifteen hundred track miles at its peak.

For those of a technical bent, the museum holds BDLX 9905 which was originally a Fairbanks/Morse Trainmaster. The Norfolk & Western made it into a de-engined slug and removed the cab. Today it still looks like a Trainmaster, but you have to know what to look for. It's a most unusual and interesting item.

Virginia Museum of Transportation, Roanoke, VA

303 Norfolk Ave SW
Roanoke, VA 24016
(540) 342-5670
www.vmt.org

Size	Rarity	Antiquity	Quality	Scope	Presentation
C	B	C	A	C	B

Land Area	**5 Acres**
Dates From	**1963**
Gauge	**Standard**
Ownership	**Private, Non-profit**
Visit Suggestion	**Mid-Day**
Locomotives	**6 Steam**
	14 Diesel
	2 Electric
	1 Other
Rolling Stock	**5 Passenger**
	7 Freight
	7 Nonrevenue
	1 Traction

It's a little disappointing to classify the Virginia Museum of Transportation as only "good." Emotionally, your author thinks it rates higher because its equipment is unique and its standard of restoration is high. But the museum is actually only of modest size and its scope is mostly limited to a single group of eastern railroads, so in honesty, we have to call it "good."

The stars of the show at the Virginia Transportation Museum, without a doubt, are Norfolk & Western 611 and 1218. The 611 is a class J 4-8-4 streamlined Northern, while the 1218 is a class A 2-6-6-4 articulated. The 611 was designed and built for the Norfolk & Western's premier passenger trains and was capable of speeds up to 110 mph, while the 1218 pulled coal trains, routinely handling 190 cars carrying 17,000 tons

Virginian number 135 is a 1956 General Electric EL-C, one of twelve made for the haulage of coal between Mullins, WV and Roanoke. It served until the wires were removed in 1962 and then went to the New Haven.

and capable of 70 mph. Both locomotives were retired from revenue service and then saw extensive rebuilding and many years of excursion train service before ending up in the museum.

For those of us who have seen pictures of the Panama Canal with little electric motors pulling ships through the locks and have wondered what those motors were like, the Virginia Museum of Transportation has one that you can see. It also has American Electric Power flatcar number 1002. While flat cars are a dime-a-dozen in most museums, number 1002 is a depressed-center car with a two hundred seventy-five ton capacity, an unusual museum holding.

Also notable at the Virginia Museum of Transportation is Virginian class EL-C number 135. Very few Virginian locomotives have been saved and the EL-C was one of their highly successful electrics. It saw service on the New Haven before being returned to Norfolk and the museum.

South Carolina Railroad Museum, Winnsboro, SC

110 Industrial Park Rd
Winnsboro, SC 29180
(803) 635-4242
www.scrm.org

Size	Rarity	Antiquity	Quality	Scope	Presentation
C	C	C	B	C	B

Land Area	6 Acres
Dates From	1973
Gauge	Standard
Ownership	Private, Non-profit
Visit Suggestion	Morning
Track	5 Miles
Locomotives	1 Steam
	6 Diesel
Rolling Stock	14 Passenger
	18 Freight
	2 Nonrevenue

A group of South Carolina railfans began collecting equipment in a small way in 1973. They established themselves as a viable non-profit organization and, in 1983, incredibly enough, a corporate donor gave

Southern Railway number XC-5 is a transfer caboose built by the Southern in the 1950s.

the museum an entire railroad. The railroad was the Rockton & Rion, an 11½ mile line that ran between Rockton Station on the Norfolk Southern, through the town of Rion, and on to a granite quarry. In the years following, the group has concentrated on rehabilitation of the line and now has five miles in use.

Interestingly, the South Carolina Railroad museum has two four-wheel coaches that were originally built by the Southern Railway to appear with a replica of the Best Friend of Charleston at the Fair of the Iron Horse held in 1927 near Baltimore. While the coaches are replicas, they have now achieved significant age on their own and are worth seeing. (A replica of the locomotive can be seen in the South Carolina State Museum, in Columbia.)

Georgia State Railroad Museum, Savannah, GA

AKA Roundhouse Railroad Museum
655 Louisville Rd
Savannah, GA 31401
(912) 651-6823
www.chsgeorgia.org

Size	Rarity	Antiquity	Quality	Scope	Presentation
C	C	B	A	C	A

Land Area	18 Acres
Dates From	1989
Gauge	Standard
Ownership	Public/Private, Non-profit
Visit Suggestion	Afternoon
Locomotives	6 Steam 5 Diesel
Rolling Stock	5 Passenger 7 Freight 4 Nonrevenue

The Georgia State Railroad Museum, also known as the Roundhouse Railroad Museum, is remarkable for its setting: the roundhouse and shops of the Georgia Central Railroad in Savannah. Thirteen original structures remain including an operational turntable. Owned by the City of Savannah, the museum is operated by the Coastal Heritage Society along with several other museums and attractions in the area.

The museum's collection isn't large, but, as is typical of state-owned museums, the level of restoration is high and almost everything in the collection has been at least cosmetically restored. The steam locomotive collection includes Central of Georgia 223, a

Two Central of Georgia business cars, the Columbus and the Atlanta occupy one end of the original Central of Georgia roundhouse at the State Railroad Museum of Georgia. Both cars are products of Pullman.

2-8-0 Consolidation, and 403, a 4-6-0 Ten-wheeler plus some smaller switch engines. Savannah & Atlanta GP35 is interesting because it appears to be one of only two pieces of equipment preserved from this 142-mile southern road.

But the shops may be the thing of greatest interest to the railfan. Although they have been cleaned and much equipment has been removed to make them safe for the public, the original structures are of real interest. In particular, the Central of Georgia shop buildings all used a single smokestack with underground connections to the shop's forges and furnaces. This brick smokestack, which survives as a local landmark and can be seen up close, originally included a set of privies (!) built into its base.

North Alabama Railroad Museum, Huntsville, AL

694 Chase Road
Huntsville, AL 35811
256-851-6276
www.northalabamarailroadmuseum.com

Size	Rarity	Antiquity	Quality	Scope	Presentation
C	C	C	C	B	B

Land Area	4 Acres
Dates From	1966
Gauge	Standard
Ownership	Private, Non-profit
Visit Suggestion	Mid-Day
Track	5 Miles
Locomotives	5 Diesel
Rolling Stock	17 Passenger 9 Freight

The North Alabama Railroad Museum was founded in 1966 as a chapter of the National Railroad Historical Society. It initially focused on the restoration and operation of a small steam engine but when, in 1985, it had the opportunity to purchase land and track, the steam locomotive was sold. The land purchased included the 1937 Chase, Alabama depot, which was

This 1926 diesel switcher was built by Alco and General Electric for service at the Union Carbide plant in Niagara Falls, New York and later at Union Carbide's plant in Sheffield, Alabama. It now lives at the North Alabama Railroad Museum.

built in 1937 to serve both the Nashville, Chattanooga & St. Louis and the Southern railroads in a spot where they happened to run side-by-side.

Today the depot has been restored and the collection has grown to thirty-one pieces, all locomotives being diesel and all Alco. One stands out: a 1926 Ingersoll Rand/Alco/GE boxcab unit donated by Union Carbide. Number 11 was initially a demonstrator, but was sold to Union Carbide in 1927 and worked in the company's New York and Alabama plants all its life before coming to the museum in 1977. It was one of the first of its kind and a precursor to the diesels that eventually took over the railroads.

Although much unrestored equipment is in the collection – as is true with all volunteer-staffed museums – it is accessible and visible to the visitor who is willing to walk the tracks and look. And an open pavilion provides shade and shelter for those who simply want to watch the Norfolk Southern roll past.

Tennessee Central Railway Museum, Nashville, TN

220 Willow St
Nashville, TN 37210
(615) 244-9001
tcry.org

Size	Rarity	Antiquity	Quality	Scope	Presentation
B	C	C	B	A	B

Land Area	7 Acres
Dates From	1989
Gauge	Standard
Ownership	Private, Non-profit
Track	83 Miles
Locomotives	9 Diesel

Rolling Stock	25 Passenger
	15 Freight
	3 Nonrevenue

The Tennessee Central Railway Museum shares yard space with the short line Nashville & Eastern, a freight railroad and host of the Music City Star commuter line. Under some circumstances this gives the railfan a chance to get close to some modern, high-horsepower diesels. The muse-

Long strings of rib-sided stainless steel cars epitomize the Tennessee Central Railroad Museum. Most appear in good condition.

um's offices, library and indoor display space is in what was once the Tennessee Central Railway's Master Mechanic's office immediately next to the yard.

The museum's focus is on passenger excursions running from Nashville to points east as far away as Monterey, Tennessee, essentially a hundred miles east. Unlike many tourist train operators, the Tennessee Central's trains are matched, rib-sided and air-conditioned lightweight equipment. The locomotive collection consists of 1950s and 1960s EMD diesels. The lightweight passenger equipment and the diesels are joined by a few freight cars and other pieces and nothing of significant rarity. Nevertheless, there are several interesting items:

- CB&Q number 4903, now Tennessee Central 2095 contains twenty-four bi-level (duplex) roomettes and four double bedrooms, resulting in a sleeping capacity of thirty-two. This "up-and-down" room arrangement was briefly popular with the railroads in the 1950s but is now uncommon in museums.
- Northern Pacific 551, now Nashville Eastern 9400, is a rib-sided dome car

- Tennessee Central 103 is an ex-Southern 10-6 sleeper rebuilt as a business car complete with an open observation platform on the rear.

Bluegrass Railroad Museum, Versailles, KY

175 Beasley Road
Versailles, KY 40383
859-873-2468
www.bgrm.org

Size	Rarity	Antiquity	Quality	Scope	Presentation
C	C	C	B	B	B

Land Area	8 Acres
Dates From	1976
Gauge	Standard
Ownership	Private, Non-profit
Visit Suggestion	Mid-Day
Track	5 Miles
Locomotives	6 Diesel
Rolling Stock	7 Passenger
	24 Freight
	3 Nonrevenue

The Bluegrass Railroad Museum is on what used to be the Lexington extension of the Louisville Southern Railroad and later became a part of the Southern Railroad's line between Lexington and St. Louis. In 1987 the museum purchased five and a half miles of the road extending east from Young's High Bridge over the Kentucky River to the edge of the city of Versailles. The bridge, now 125 years old, remains standing, but has been out of service since 1983. Unfortunately, almost half of the museum's collection remains stranded on the west side of the bridge and, to date, money has not been available to construct additional storage track in Versailles or to pay for trucking of the cars past the gap. Land, however, is available and the stranded rolling stock is accessible to visitors. Ask for directions.

Arguably the most interesting car on the Bluegrass roster is Nashville,

Norfolk & Western 675, an EMD GP9, poses on a small wood trestle at the Bluegrass Railroad Museum.

Chattanooga and St. Louis number 90130, a dynamometer car designed to measure locomotive performance in actual operation. Number 90130 was built in 1916 by American Car & Foundry and served on the NC&StL until it was bought by the Louisville & Nashville in 1937. In 1957 the L&N converted it to a camp car for use by track maintenance crews and in 1970 it was listed as scrap. A private individual bought the car and re-sold it to the Bluegrass Railroad Museum in 1978. Restoration efforts continue.

Railway Museum of Greater Cincinnati, Covington, KY

315 West Southern Ave
Covington, KY 41015
cincirailmuseum.org

Size	Rarity	Antiquity	Quality	Scope	Presentation
C	C	C	C	B	C

Land Area	3 Acres
Dates From	1975
Gauge	Standard
Ownership	Private, Non-profit
Visit Suggestion	Afternoon
Locomotives	5 Diesel
Rolling Stock	24 Passenger
	11 Freight

With the formation of Amtrak in 1971, the common carrier roads ceased passenger service, making many cars surplus. A number of people purchased cars and used them for some time in private service, running on the back of Amtrak passenger trains. Then Amtrak changed the rules, signifi-

PRR E-8 number 5888 posed with Pullman sleeper Castle View and B&O bay-window caboose C2873 at the Railway Museum of Greater Cincinnati.

cantly upgrading its standards and requiring repairs and improvements that were often beyond the financial reach of private car owners. An operating group in the Cincinnati area decided to change their emphasis to collection and restoration and thus the current Railway Museum of Greater Cincinnati came into being.

Over the years, the museum has stored and displayed its equipment at several sites including New York Central's Riverside Yard, Baltimore & Ohio's Storrs Yard and Louisville & Nashville's Latonia Yard. When, in 1991, the museum again lost its lease, it chose to purchase the land it was on rather than move. Today it lives at the junction of the historic Kentucky Central and Louisville, Cincinnati & Lexington Railroads on what is now CSX track. As the crow flies, Covington, Kentucky and the Latonia yard are some three miles south of the Ohio River and the city of Cincinnati.

Because of its heritage, the museum focuses heavily on passenger equipment and mostly on the Pennsylvania and Baltimore & Ohio railroads. The freight car collection is growing, but as of this writing the items of most interest in the collection include:

- Pennsylvania Railroad E-8 number 5888 is prominently displayed along with some lightweight rib-side passenger cars
- Three cars from the Pennsylvania *Fleet of Modernism* of 1939: sleepers Cascade Gardens and Cascade Heights and round-end observation/sleeper Metropolitan View. Cascade Gardens has been restored while the other two await work, but all three are still of significant interest.
- A five-car Baltimore & Ohio passenger "train" (not necessarily coupled together) consisting of three heavyweight and two lightweight cars with the lightweight observation *Chicago* bringing up the rear.

Latonia Yard was built as a working freight yard and there are drawbacks to its use as a museum. There is relatively little room between the tracks and it isn't easy to see some of the collection. Be prepared to put in some effort and maybe get a little dirty if you want to tour everything.

Northern Ohio Railway Museum, Seville, OH

5515 Buffham Road
Seville, OH 44273
330-769-5501
www.trainweb.org/norm

Size	Rarity	Antiquity	Quality	Scope	Presentation
C	C	C	B	C	B

Land Area	30 Acres
Dates From	1976
Gauge	Standard
Ownership	Private, Non-profit
Visit Suggestion	Mid-Day
Track	1 Mile
Locomotives	3 Electric 1 Other
Rolling Stock	9 Freight 9 Nonrevenue 25 Traction

The Northern Ohio Railway Museum originated in 1965 with the purchase of a single caboose. In 1977 two miles of former Cleveland, Southwestern & Columbus right-of-way was purchased and in 1984 thirty acres of land adjacent to the tracks was bought allowing space for a storage yard and barns.

Cleveland Railway number 225, a 1914 product of Kuhlman, poses with a Ford Model T. The two restored vehicles are contemporaries.

As it exists today, the museum has come to concentrate entirely on electric railroads. Neither steam nor diesel locomotives appear in its roster and about three-quarters of its equipment originally served within fifty miles or so of Cleveland, but the Cleveland area and most of northern Ohio has a particularly rich electric railroad history and there is much to be seen. For instance:

- Cleveland Railway number 1225 (pictured above) is a 1914 Kuhlman center-entrance rapid transit car

- Cleveland Transit numbers 161 and 172 are Pullman "air-porters," built in 1967 and 1970 for service on the line to Cleveland Hopkins International Airport.
- Toledo Edison number 2 is a fifty-ton steeple-cab locomotive built by the Differential Steel Car Company in 1924.

Mahoning Valley Railroad Heritage Association, Youngstown, OH

1340 Poland Ave
Youngstown, OH 44551
330-792-0339
www.mvrha.org

Size	Rarity	Antiquity	Quality	Scope	Presentation
C	A	C	C	C	B

Land Area	**3 Acres**
Dates From	**1985**
Gauge	**Standard**
Ownership	**Private, Non-profit**
Visit Suggestion	**Afternoon**
Locomotives	**3 Steam**
	1 Diesel
	1 Other
Rolling Stock	**3 Passenger**
	9 Freight
	1 Nonrevenue

In terms of its collection size, the Mahoning Valley Railroad Heritage Association is the smallest museum listed in this book and would probably not be listed at all except for the rarity of its equipment. Six of its nine freight cars are directly related to the steel industry including hot metal cars, a ladle car, a mold car and an ore car. For those interested in the steel industry and railroad activity inside the steel plants, this is like finding gold.

In addition to the steel industry collection, the Mahoning Valley has a Baldwin 0-6-0 and two 0-4-0 steam locomotives, one of them a fireless "teakettle." The passenger collection consists of a Pennsylvania Railroad RPO and two

Pittsburgh & Lake Erie 506, a "hot metal car", was built in December 1950.

World War II era troop sleepers. They are joined by a varied collection of signals and other artifacts.

Access to the collection is limited and available only by appointment. Call ahead if you want to see these cars.

Mad River & NKP Railroad Museum, Bellevue, OH

233 York St
Bellevue, OH 44811
(419) 483-2222
www.madrivermuseum.org

Size	Rarity	Antiquity	Quality	Scope	Presentation
C	B	C	B	B	B+

Land Area	4 Acres
Dates From	1976
Gauge	Standard
Ownership	Private, Non-profit
Visit Suggestion	Afternoon

Locomotives	3 Steam
	9 Diesel
	1 Electric
	2 Other
Rolling Stock	15 Passenger
	14 Freight
	10 Nonrevenue

Bellevue, Ohio is located about halfway between Cleveland and Toledo on track that was once a New York Central freight line between Cleveland and Toledo. The museum is just west of the spot where that line crossed the Pennsylvania's north-south line to Sandusky and the

Baltimore & Ohio wagon-top caboose C2424 has been restored to its original B&O colors and is on display at the Mad River and NKP Museum.

Nickel Plate's east-west line between Cleveland and both Chicago and St. Louis. Land adjacent to the track was leased in 1975. Two display tracks were built, the Wheeling & Lake Erie depot from Curtice, Ohio was purchased and moved onto the museum's site, and the museum opened to the public in 1976.

Now, more than thirty years later, the Mad River and NKP Museum advertises itself as the largest in Ohio. Not only is that claim true, the museum has put significant effort into making visitors welcome and comfortable with paved walks, reasonable spacing between tracks, and neatly groomed grounds. Further, there are a number of interesting, significant and unusual pieces to be seen:
• The Mad River Railroad's *Sandusky*, a replica 0-4-0 locomotive built by the Baltimore & Ohio circa 1903 for the 1904 Chicago World's Fair

- Nickel Plate 329, an ALCO RSD-12 in Nickel Plate black with yellow striping and with the cab frequently open to visitors
- Nickel Plate X50041, a dynamometer car
- Nickel Plate 900, a GP30 in black-and-yellow
- Milwaukee Road 740, a Fairbanks/Morse H12-44 switcher in the road's colorful grey-over-orange paint
- A very unusual Pennsylvania RR side-arm car pusher from the Sandusky docks
- Chicago Burlington & Quincy coach number 4714, the Silver Dome. This car was the first dome car built and at the time of its construction, was experimental. It predates the later and more famous Budd domes.

Hoosier Valley Railroad Museum, North Judson, IN

507 Mulberry Street
North Judson, IN 46366
(574) 896-3950
www.hoosiervalley.org

Size	Rarity	Antiquity	Quality	Scope	Presentation
C	C	C	B	B	B

Land Area	7 Acres
Dates From	1988
Gauge	Standard
Ownership	Private, Non-profit
Visit Suggestion	Afternoon
Track	1 Mile
Locomotives	2 Steam
	4 Diesel
Rolling Stock	3 Passenger
	23 Freight
	5 Nonrevenue

North Judson, Indiana was once a rail hub. It was served by the Pennsylvania, the Erie, the Chesapeake & Ohio and the New York Central with crossings and interchange yards abounding. The Erie became part of the Erie-Lackawanna, which became part of Conrail.

Erie-Lackawanna 310 is a 1947 Alco S1. It sits in front of the North Judson depot with Bessemer & Lake Erie caboose 1989,

Conrail sold the line that passed through North Judson and it went through a series of short-line operators before finally being abandoned in 2004. One mile of the track was donated to the Hoosier Valley museum, while rail was removed from the rest.

In 1961 the C&O donated Kanawha number 2789 to a steam preservation group and it was placed on display in a park in Peru, Indiana. In 1988 it was moved to North Judson and placed in the care of the Hoosier Valley Museum. If and when money can be found, 2789 will be restored to operating condition.

The class K4 Kanawha is, by far, the most impressive piece in the museum's collection. The giant super-power steam locomotive was built in 1947 by the American Locomotive Company for dual passenger/freight use through the mountains. A thoroughly "modern" steamer, it has a welded boiler and roller bearings.

Although less imposing, the museum has an unnumbered EMC Model 40 4-wheel diesel switcher. A rare model, built before the Electromotive Corporation was taken over by General Motors, this ex-Calumet Steel unit will be of interest to those who appreciate "critters."

And the museum has a fully operating signal system and an ex-Indiana Harbor Belt mechanical interlocking tower that is currently undergoing restoration.

National New York Central Railroad Museum, Elkhart, IN

721 S Main Street
Elkhart, IN 46516
(574) 294-3001
www.nycrrmuseum.org

Size	Rarity	Antiquity	Quality	Scope	Presentation
C	C	C	C	C	B

Land Area	4 Acres
Dates From	1987
Gauge	Standard
Ownership	Public
Visit Suggestion	Mid-Day
Locomotives	1 Steam
	1 Diesel
	1 Electric
Rolling Stock	7 Passenger
	15 Freight
	6 Nonrevenue

One would expect a museum dedicated to the New York Central to be in New York or Chicago or maybe in Buffalo near the now-vacant and decaying art deco depot. But it isn't. The National New York Central Railroad Museum is located across the tracks from the Elkhart, Indiana Amtrak station. Appropriately, it is on the old New York Central mainline between New York and Chicago and, incidentally, at the point where two historic rail lines diverge (both still in occasional use): the Michigan Southern and the Elkhart & Western. In 1852 the Michigan Southern, later to become part of the New York Central, was the first railroad to reach Chicago from the east. The Elkhart & Western was completed in 1893. Designed to provide competition in the one-railroad town of Elkhart, it was soon taken over by the Vanderbilts, ending all competitive possibilities.

In the 1980s a group of ex-railroaders and railfans began to collect equipment. One member of the group owned

There were once six hundred New York Central Mohawks, massive high-speed freight haulers with sixty-nine inch drivers and with the ability to pinch-hit as necessary in passenger service at 80 mph. Two survive. The newer (built in 1940) is at the National New York Central Museum in Elkhart, Indiana.

the ex-New York Central depot and, across the tracks, the freight house. In 1987 the land was sold to the City of Elkhart and the museum was formed. Some years later, an ex-Pennsylvania Railroad GG1 was traded to the Age of Steam Museum in Dallas, Texas for the New York Central Mohawk, which had been masquerading as a Texas & Pacific 4-8-2 Mountain. Still later, a second GG1 was acquired. In the following years, the City has developed the museum as a tourist attraction and as a site importantly related to its deep railroading history.

Today the New York Central Railroad Museum centers around three massive locomotives, all well worth a visit:
- New York Central 4-8-2 L-3a Mohawk, number 3001. Very few New York Central steam locomotives have been preserved and having an example as modern and powerful as the 3001 is a real treat. It was built by Alco in 1940.
- New York Central EMD E8 diesel-electric locomotive, number 4085 in lightning stripe paint. Prime passenger power

for the Twentieth Century Limited in the 1940s and 1950s. 4085 dates from 1953.

- Pennsylvania Railroad GG1 electric locomotive number 4882 wearing Penn Central black and the "two worms in love" logo. While the GG1 is a little out of place in Indiana, it is still good to see what most would agree is the most successful electric locomotive ever built.

Whitewater Valley Railroad, Connersville, IN

5 Eastern Ave
Connersville, IN 47331
(765) 825-2054
www.whitewatervalleyrr.org

Size	Rarity	Antiquity	Quality	Scope	Presentation
C	C	C	B	C	C

Land Area	3 Acres
Dates From	1972
Gauge	Standard
Ownership	Private, Non-profit
Visit Suggestion	Afternoon
Track	19 Miles
Locomotives	3 Steam
	10 Diesel
	1 Other
Rolling Stock	13 Passenger
	23 Freight
	1 Nonrevenue

The Whitewater Valley Railroad built track into Connersville, Indiana arriving in 1867, and continued north another twenty miles to Hagerstown in 1868. The line became part of the Big Four (the Cleveland, Cincinnati, Chicago & St. Louis, a subsidiary of the New York Central) in 1890 and was merged into the Central in 1930. Passenger service ended in 1933, but freight service continued with decreasing frequency until a washout isolated part of the line in 1974.

In 1972 a non-profit group of railfans took up the then-dormant Whitewater Valley name. When Conrail removed four miles of rail in 1976, he group went to work and, in 1983, was able

Cincinnati Union Terminal number 25, a 108-ton product of Lima-Hamilton, and Baltimore and Ohio Caboose C2232 on the Whitewater Valley Railroad. The diesel is lettered for the Whitewater Valley.

to purchase eighteen miles of line running south from Connersville to Metamora, Indiana.

The Whitewater Valley Railroad holds several interesting pieces including a Baltimore & Ohio wagon top caboose and a Pennsylvania Railroad N8 cabin car (both in the process of restoration at this writing).

Also of interest and somewhat unusual is the museum's collection of diesels, which features five units that bracket the ill-fated mergers of Baldwin Locomotive Works with Lima and Hamilton. Patapsco & Black Rivers 335, a 1000-horsepower switcher built by Baldwin in 1949 begins the series. Three Lima-Hamilton switchers built in 1950 and 1951 are sandwiched in the middle and Patapsco & Black Rivers 346, a 1951 DS-4-4-1000 built by Baldwin-Lima-Hamilton in 1951 brings up the rear. It's an interesting comparison. Very few Lima-Hamilton diesels were produced and these three could be the only survivors.

The Whitewater Valley also has a preserved interlocking tower. While several museums have such towers, this one is a little special because it is relatively complete, because it was never automated and thus retains its mechanical apparatus, and because it is probably a hundred twenty-five years old. Originally built to protect the crossing of the Cincinnati & Southern Ohio River Railway and the Big Four, the tower has been moved to a road crossing a half-mile south of the museum's yard and shop on Indiana Route 121.

Indiana Railway Museum, French Lick, IN

1 Monon Drive
French Lick, IN 47432
800-74-TRAIN
www.indianarailwaymuseum.org

Size	Rarity	Antiquity	Quality	Scope	Presentation
B	C	C	B	B	C

Land Area	4 Acres
Dates From	1961
Gauge	Standard
Ownership	Private, Non-profit
Visit Suggestion	Mid-Day
Track	10 Miles
Locomotives	3 Steam
	11 Diesel
	1 Electric
	1 Other
Rolling Stock	28 Passenger
	58 Freight
	1 Traction

The Indiana Railway Museum was first formed in 1961 in Westport, Indiana, a small town some sixty miles west of Cincinnati. It moved to nearby Greensburg in 1971 and then moved again, this time in 1978 to French Lick. The move to French Lick resulted from the museum's purchase of sixteen miles of Southern Railway track extending from West Baden through French Lick and southwest to Dubois. The museum has been there ever since.

The size of the Indiana Railway Museum's collection might justify its rating as "really good," but unfortunately much of the equipment is stored inaccessible to the public and to visiting railfans and more can be seen only with a significant hike along a storage track. Possibly the most

Indiana Railroad Pullman car number 345, the Indianapolis, stands at the station in French Lick.

unique piece in the collection is a small electric locomotive built in 1920 by General Electric for the Brooklyn Street Railway. Even though it remains unrestored, it's worth seeing. The passenger collection is also of interest since it includes five heavyweight business cars (from the Erie, two from the Seaboard, and one each from the Monon, and the Lehigh Valley) as well as the Pullman-built lightweight observation car *Samuel Rea*.

Fox River Trolley Museum, South Elgin, IL

361 South LaFox Street
South Elgin, IL 60177
(847) 697-4676
www.foxtrolley.org

Size	Rarity	Antiquity	Quality	Scope	Presentation
C	C	C	A	C	B

Land Area	6 Acres
Dates From	1966

Gauge	Standard
Ownership	Private, Non-profit
Visit Suggestion	Mid-Day
Track	2 Miles
Locomotives	2 Diesel
	2 Electric
Rolling Stock	2 Freight
	3 Nonrevenue
	19 Traction

The Fox River Trolley Museum operates on track that was first laid down by the Elgin, Aurora and Southern Traction Company in 1896. After a 1906 merger with the Aurora, Elgin & Chicago, it regained its independence as the Aurora, Elgin and Fox River Electric Company.

Chicago, North Shore & Milwaukee number 756 is a "silverliner." Unable to afford stainless steel ribs to decorate their cars, the railroad developed a way of painting them to simulate what the steam road competition was doing for real.

The rise of the automobile and truck brought passenger service to an end in 1935 but the railroad continued as freight-only, its largest customer being the State Mental Hospital in Elgin. When that hospital stopped burning coal for heat in 1971, the line closed and the tracks were abandoned.

While all of this was going on, a group of railfans had purchased seven trolley cars and interurbans and had bought a plot of land adjacent to the AE&FR, opening as a museum in 1966. Today the museum's holdings have grown and a mile and a half of ex-AE&FR track is used for demonstration rides.

The Fox River Trolley Museum's holdings include several interesting pieces:

- Chicago Surface Lines number 6 is a street railway post office car built in 1891. Once a year the South Elgin post office still ceremonially staffs it as a branch office.
- Chicago, Aurora & Elgin number 20 is said to be America's oldest operating interurban
- Chicago, South Shore & South Bend cars number 7 and 14 are sister cars, but number 14 was lengthened in 1925 by the CSS&SB, which cut it and most other CSS&SB cars in half and welded in a seventeen foot addition. Car 7 was not lengthened, so the contrast between the two illustrates what can be done by a creative and skilled shop.
- Chicago Rapid Transit 5001 is a three-car articulated set, a prototype which was built and tested, ultimately leading to the CTA 6000 car series.

Oklahoma Railway Museum, Oklahoma City, OK

3400 N.E. Grand Blvd
Oklahoma City, OK 73111
405-424-8222
www.oklahomarailwaymuseum.org

Size	Rarity	Antiquity	Quality	Scope	Presentation
C	C	C	B	C	B

Land Area	5 Acres
Dates From	1997
Gauge	Standard
Ownership	Private, Non-profit
Visit Suggestion	Mid-Day
Track	3 Miles
Locomotives	1 Steam
	8 Diesel
	1 Other

Rolling Stock	9 Passenger
	19 Freight
	2 Nonrevenue

The biggest and best of the railroad museums in this book were founded in the 1930s, 1940s, 1950s or 1960s and have had a half-century or more to grow and develop. The Oklahoma Railway Museum is an exception. A

Santa Fe number 90 is an EMD FP45 at the Oklahoma Railroad Museum.

relative newcomer to the field, the organization behind it was created in 1972 and the museum itself opened in 1997. A great deal has been accomplished in that time.

The Oklahoma Railway Museum has a number of interesting pieces in its collection:

- Atchison, Topeka & Santa Fe number 90 is an EMD FP45 built in 1969 and displayed in the red and silver warbonnet paint scheme. The FP45s were first built for passenger service, but were relegated to freight when Amtrak took over the passenger trains in 1971.
- Chicago, Burlington & Quincy caboose 14107 was originally built as Burlington & Missouri River number 10. Built by Wells & French in 1878, it is believed to be the oldest Burlington caboose in existence.
- San Luis Valley M-300 is a railbus. Built originally for passenger service, it turned out to be too light to perform switching duties, so it was modified with the addition of a truck axle in the hopes that rubber tires would improve traction. The experiment was a failure since the tires wore out very quickly, but the M-300 still exists. It's known as "the mouse," partly because of its grey color, but also partly in memory of the hordes of mice that used to live in it.

Museum of the American Railroad, Frisco, TX

6455 Page Street
Frisco, TX 75034
(972) 292-5665
www.museumoftheamericanrailroad.org

Size	Rarity	Antiquity	Quality	Scope	Presentation
C	A	C	A	B	Not rated

Land Area	12 Acres
Dates From	1963
Gauge	Standard
Ownership	Private, Non-profit
Locomotives	4 Steam 8 Diesel 1 Electric 1 Other
Rolling Stock	16 Passenger 8 Freight 1 Nonrevenue

Once known as the Age of Steam Museum, what is now the Museum of the American Railroad began as a display at the 1963 State Fair of Texas in Dallas. Two steam locomotives and a transplanted 1905 yard office/ depot were displayed on the fairgrounds adjacent to the Texas & Pacific tracks. In the years that followed, volunteers staffed the exhibit on weekends and performed simple maintenance while occasional acquisitions were made. In 1989 ownership of the collection was transferred to the volunteer organization, the Southwest Railroad Historical Society.

By 2005 the museum, renamed the Museum of the American Railroad, had completely outgrown its original 1½ acre site and was looking for new space. The City of Frisco, similarly, was looking for an attraction that would celebrate its heritage and had space available. Ground was broken on the new site in

2011 and the move is under way as this is written. Because the museum is temporarily closed and because its site remains under development, we have not rated the Museum of the American Railroad in the "presentation" category. But we can still review and discuss the collection.

Atchison Topeka & Santa Fe motorcar M-160 is shown with Missouri-Kansas-Texas number 3, a heavyweight diner. M-160 was built by Brill in 1931; the diner by ACF in 1937. Both are at the Museum of the American Railroad in Frisco, Texas.

While the Museum of the American Railroad, even in its new location, may not be the largest railroad museum in the country, the people who run it have done an excellent job of gathering together some of the largest and most impressive locomotives anywhere. The best of the collection includes:

- St Louis-San Francisco number 4501, a huge 4-8-4 Northern built by Baldwin in 1940
- Union Pacific 4-8-8-4 number 4018, a Big Boy
- St Louis–San Francisco number 1625, a 1918 Alco 2-10-0 decapod
- Union Pacific number 6913, a DD-40-X "Centennial"
- Atchison, Topeka & Santa Fe number 105, an SDFP-45
- Atchison, Topeka & Santa Fe number 59L, an Alco PA built in 1948 (and one of only two surviving PA units in the USA). The 59L is being restored and, at this writing, is not accessible to the public.
- Atchison Topeka & Santa Fe motorcar No. M-160 (a flat-faced doodlebug in warbonnet paint)
- Pennsylvania Railroad GG-1 number 4906 (a long way from home)

Galveston Railroad Museum, Galveston, TX

2602 Santa Fe Place
Galveston, TX 77550
(409) 765-5700
www.galvestonrrmuseum.com

Size	Rarity	Antiquity	Quality	Scope	Presentation
C	C	C	B	B	A

Land Area	8 Acres
Dates From	1983
Gauge	Standard
Ownership	Private, Non-profit
Visit Suggestion	Afternoon
Track	1 Mile
Locomotives	3 Steam
	3 Diesel
	1 Other
Rolling Stock	15 Passenger
	11 Freight
	3 Nonrevenue

Galveston RR Museum is located on Galveston Island in what was originally Galveston Union Station. The station building and the display tracks are only a little more than a mile from the Gulf of Mexico and only a block from the place where cruise ships dock between the island and the mainland. It's a very urban environment and one entirely appropriate to trains. Unfortunately, it's also one that is very exposed to weather. In September 2008, hurricane Ike flooded the site completely, causing major damage and extensive closure of the museum. Full reopening occurred only after four years' work, in 2012.

Galveston Union Station was originally built as two separate eight-story art-deco buildings, the first completed in 1915. In 1932 the second building was completed and the space between the buildings was filled in with a ten-story tower, making the two structures into a single, much larger one.

At one point the station served the Santa Fe, the Missouri-Kansas-Texas, the Missouri Pacific, and the Southern Pacific. Its last pas-

Santa Fe F7A units 315 and 316 are newly rebuilt and repainted at the Galveston Railroad Museum.

senger train left in 1967 and the building sat idle until it was purchased by a private developer. Today the city and county occupy the upper floors and the railroad museum lives on the ground floor. The waiting room and ticket windows have been restored to their original appearance, making a suitable adjunct to the equipment stored outside on the five station tracks.

Beyond doubt the stars of the show at the Galveston Railroad Museum are the twin F7A diesels. Even though F7 locomotives are common in museums and warbonnet paint schemes abound, this matched pair with consecutive numbers is unusual and worth seeing. Southern Pacific 100, a Budd RDC car is iconic and also interesting. Three smallish steam locomotives and a Fairbanks-Morse H20-44 diesel round out the power roster. All are displayed with a group of passenger and freight cars and with a Rock Island crane, tender and idler car.

Pueblo Railway Museum, Pueblo, CO

201 West B Street
Pueblo, CO 81003
719-251-5024
www.pueblorailway.org

Size	Rarity	Antiquity	Quality	Scope	Presentation
C	B	C	B	B	B

Land Area	5 Acres
Dates From	2003
Gauge	Standard
Ownership	Private, Non-profit
Visit Suggestion	Afternoon
Locomotives	1 Steam 6 Diesel 3 Other
Rolling Stock	2 Passenger 12 Freight 5 Nonrevenue 1 Traction

The Pueblo Railway Museum, located next to restored Pueblo Union Station, has several interesting holdings. First and foremost is AT&SF number 2912, a 1944 Baldwin 4-8-4 Northern, which was undergoing cosmetic restoration at the time this was written. The 2912 is unusual in that it rides

This strange looking vehicle is a USDOT experimental unit known as the Rohr. Riding on (and hovering above) a single vertical rail, it was powered by a linear induction motor embedded in the track.

on huge 80-inch driving wheels and was once reputedly clocked at 120 mph pulling fifteen passenger cars in New Mexico.

The 2912 is joined by a number of lightweight passenger cars, a small amount of freight equipment, a single trolley car, and several post-war diesels, three of which are operational. But the most fascinating of the museum's holdings are three experimental units:

- The Rohr Aero train, a linear-induction motor powered monorail hovercraft designed to carry sixty people at 150 mph. It is said that the Rohr was a technical success but an economic failure. Operating costs were beyond the levels that any passenger market would support.
- The Grumman TLRV, a rail-mounted vehicle that was reputedly designed, built and used for aerodynamic testing as part of the space shuttle program. The history of this unit is clouded but some feel that it was rail mounted and registered to the US Department of Transportation in the 1970s to shield its true purpose from the competing Soviets.
- The Garrett, which ran on two rails powered by another linear induction motor together with two Pratt & Whitney J52 jet engines. Running on specially built track at the US Department of Transportation's Colorado Test Site, the Garrett reached 258.4 mph setting a world rail speed record at the time.

Unfortunately none of these vehicles are routinely displayed, but they can usually be seen on request.

Utah State Railroad Museum, Ogden, UT

2501 Wall Ave
Ogden, UT 84401
866-379-9599
theunionstation.org

Size	Rarity	Antiquity	Quality	Scope	Presentation
C	C	C	B	B	A

Land Area	2 Acres
Dates From	1978
Gauge	Standard
Ownership	Public
Visit Suggestion	Afternoon
Locomotives	3 Steam
	10 Diesel
	1 Other
Rolling Stock	5 Passenger
	19 Freight
	5 Nonrevenue
	15 Traction

A modest museum, the Utah State Railroad Museum displays more than two dozen prototype pieces from its collection, and displays them reasonably well. Some are under roof but outdoors and others are exposed to the elements. All are shown at historic Ogden Union Station immediately next to a working railroad track.

UP number 26 is an 8500 horsepower gas turbine built in 1961 and retired in 1970. The Utah State Railroad Museum displays number 26, one of two turbine survivors.

Ogden has had a union station since 1889 but the current building dates from 1924 when it replaced an earlier station that was destroyed by fire. When passenger service ended in 1977, the Union Pacific leased the station to the city of Ogden for use as museum space and it has served in that capacity ever since. In 1988 the State of Utah designated the Union Station as the official Utah State Railroad Museum.

While the museum does a reasonably good job of displaying its collection and even though restoration of all the pieces is incomplete (no museum is ever done with restoration), the museum suffers from a lack of scope. With minor exception, everything shown relates to western railroading in the post-war years.

Of special note are three Union Pacific locomotives: 4-8-4 number 833 (with its elephant ears still in place), DDAX40 Centennial number 6916, and gas turbine number 26. The museum also displays Union Pacific rotary snowplow number 900061 with a Vanderbilt cylindrical tender and an impressive 250-ton Union Pacific diesel wrecking crane.

Arizona Railway Museum, Chandler, AZ

330 E. Ryan Road
Chandler, AZ 85286
(480) 821-1108
www.azrymuseum.org

Size	Rarity	Antiquity	Quality	Scope	Presentation
C	C	C	B	B	A

Land Area	7 Acres
Dates From	1983
Gauge	Mixed
Ownership	Private, Non-profit
Visit Suggestion	Mid-Day
Locomotives	2 Steam 3 Diesel 1 Other
Rolling Stock	15 Passenger 19 Freight 3 Nonrevenue 1 Traction

The Arizona Railway Museum was founded in 1983 by five railfans who saw a need for preservation of local railroad history. A nonprofit corporation was created and, with it, the group leased space in a city

Union Pacific 4815, a newly-restored diner known as the City of Chandler, sits in the yard at the Arizona Railway Museum. It was built in 1949 by American Car & Foundry.

park, taking over the restoration and maintenance of Southern Pacific 2562, a 1906 Baldwin 2-8-0 Consolidation, which had been rapidly deteriorating under city care. Three display tracks were built and by 1996 they had been filled with purchased and donated equipment. By 2003 two more tracks had been built and filled, occupying all of the available land so, in 2006, the museum moved to another city park where a larger plot of land could be leased, more than doubling the museum's size.

As one of the newest railroad museum in the country, a great deal has been accomplished in a relatively short time, particularly considering the fact that the era of railroad bankruptcies and massive equipment selloffs is over. The Arizona Railway Museum is the only museum in the state with a significant display collection,

The collection is stored outdoors, little or no cover being required in the Arizona weather. Heat, however, is a factor and the Arizona Railway Museum closes during the summer months. Storage space for the collection is generous and the equipment is displayed on tracks that are nicely spaced, making viewing easy.

As might be expected, the museum's collection is mostly western and mostly post-1930. There are, however, some pieces of particular interest:

- Southern Pacific 2562, the 1906 Baldwin 2-8-0 Consolidation mentioned above, originally donated to the City of Chandler by the Southern Pacific.
- An unusual car mover manufactured by the Marmon Transmotive Company, the Model 9000 "Switchmaster" was designed for low-volume movements normally in an industrial setting. It's a strange looking beast and worth seeing.
- Southern Pacific 7241 is a three door horse car with end doors, built by St. Louis Car Company in 1937. While horse cars aren't unique, they are uncommon enough in museums to be interesting.
- Toronto Transit 4607 is a PCC car. PCC cars, 1930s electric trolleys, are far from unusual and some are still in revenue service. One does not expect to find a PCC in Arizona where electric transit was uncommon.

Mount Rainier Scenic Railroad, Elbe, WA

54124 Mountain Hwy E
Elbe, WA 98330
(360) 492-5588
www.mrsr.com

Size	Rarity	Antiquity	Quality	Scope	Presentation
B	B	C	B	C	B

Land Area	18 Acres
Dates From	1980
Gauge	Standard
Ownership	Private, Non-profit
Visit Suggestion	Afternoon
Track	6 Miles
Locomotives	7 Steam
	4 Diesel
Rolling Stock	16 Passenger
	35 Freight
	10 Nonrevenue

In 1980 the Milwaukee Road sold its 66-mile branch from Tacoma to Morton, Washington to the Weyerhaeuser Timber Company. A collector of antique railroad equipment gained permission from Weyerhaeuser to run trains on the line and the Mount Rainier

Willamette Shay number 2 (ex-Rayonier) leads a Climax and a Heisler at Park Junction on the Mt. Rainier Scenic Railroad

Scenic Railroad was born. In 1994 Weyerhaeuser closed the line, sold a portion of it to the City of Tacoma, and donated the rest. The city continues to own the right-of-way and the track and leases the segment between Mineral and Elbe to the Mount Rainier Scenic Railroad.

As of this writing, the Mount Rainier Scenic Railroad has two Shays, two Heislers and a Climax, all of the three-truck variety. It also has three 2-8-2 Mikado rod engines, one each from Baldwin, Alco and Porter. Six of the eight are either in operating condition or close to it. This museum is the only place in the country (and probably in the world) where all three kinds of geared steam are present and all are operational.

The impressive list of steam locomotives is joined by four diesels, an NW2 and two RSD-1s and a Northern Pacific F9.

Except for the passenger equipment and the diesels, the museum is very oriented toward logging. The freight equipment collection is dominated by a string of eighteen ex-Chehalis Western, nee-Weyerhaeuser Timber skeleton log cars. As an adjunct to its displays and train rides, Mount Rainier Scenic is in the process of opening a logging museum.

Museum of Alaska Transportation and Industry, Wasilla, AK

3800 West Museum Drive
Wasilla, AK 99654
(907) 376-1211
www.museumofalaska.org

Size	Rarity	Antiquity	Quality	Scope	Presentation
C	C	C	B	B	B

Land Area	20 Acres
Dates From	1967
Gauge	Standard
Ownership	Private, Non-profit
Visit Suggestion	Afternoon

The Air Progress Museum opened in 1967 near Anchorage International Airport with, oddly, six retired troop carrier cars prominent in its collection. The cars were filled with exhibits of the museum's smaller items and were actually used for some time to carry the museum itself to Fairbanks and other towns on the Alaska Railroad. A fire forced closure of the museum in 1973.

In 1976 the remnants of the Air Progress Museum re-opened on the State Fair Grounds. The collection grew and the museum became the Transportation Museum of Alaska. In the 1980s, oil prosperity brought a measure of government funding, but the money dried up after a few years and the museum is now independent. In 1992 land was purchased in Wasilla (an Anchorage suburb) and the museum gained a permanent home.

Visitors to the Museum of Alaska Transportation and Industry will see that it contains an interesting variety of non-rail vehicles including cars, trucks, snow vehicles, boats and airplanes, many specially adapted for local conditions. But the rail collection is what interests us most for purposes of this book.

Being where the museum is, and considering transportation costs, the rail collection is almost entirely made up of Alaska Railroad equipment. The signature piece is AKRR 1500, a 1952 EMD F7A, freshly painted, sporting a snow-plow under its nose, and located next to the main entrance of the museum. Also of interest are AKRR number 1000, a 1944 Alco RS1

In the 1960s the Sportsman Lodge in Whittier, Alaska had no road connection to the territory's interior, but there was a branch of the Alaska Railroad and a rail tunnel, so the lodge bought this charming little railbus to run through the tunnel hauling guests to and from the property. Known as the "ice worm," the bus now can be seen at the Museum of Alaska Transportation and Industry in Wasilla near Anchorage.

with an unusually low chopped nose and 1718, a 1952 EMD MRS-1 military service locomotive, also in fresh paint. Several other locomotives by Baldwin and General Electric, joined by an Industrial Brownhoist crane and a Jordan spreader are mixed in with freight and passenger cars to complete the scene.

Some Great Rides

This is a book about railroad museums, not about train rides. But the line between them can be blurry at times, especially since many museums have found that train rides can be a significant source of revenue. Some of the rides offered are so outstanding that it's hard to ignore them. So here are the ones I consider greatest.

A great ride, by the way, requires four things to my way of thinking:
- Significant length – more than just a mile or two
- Interesting or, better yet, historic equipment
- Great or historic scenery
- Rules that allow riding in a vestibule, on a rear platform, in an open car or, best of all, in the locomotive.

As with the museums, the great rides are listed in zip code sequence.

Cass Scenic Railroad State Park, Cass, WV

Front Street
Cass, WV 24927
(304) 456-4300
www.cassrailroad.com

Length	Gauge	Usual Power
11 miles	Standard	Steam

Throughout the nineteen century, well into the twentieth and even into the twenty-first, West Virginia has been heavily forested and its lumbering and paper industries have been major sources of jobs and money. Starting in 1900, rails were laid up into the mountains from an interchange with the Western Maryland in the village of Cass. But the rails weren't laid to haul

136

merchandise, they existed to feed the giant lumber and pulp mills that had been built in Cass by the West Virginia Pulp and Paper Company. At the peak, some one hundred-forty miles of mainline and branches were in operation and it is estimated that two hundred fifty miles were built in total. In 1910 the railroad became known as the Greenbrier, Cheat & Elk.

Cass Scenic Railroad number 11 is a three-tuck Lima shay, built in 1923. Originally sold to the Hutchinson Lumber Company, it saw service as Feather River Railway number 3 and came to Cass in 1997. Fully operational, it hauls trains up and down the mountain on a daily basis.

In 1926 the Western Maryland purchased seventy-four miles of the line and used it to haul coal. But as the demand for coal waned and as the old-growth timber was cut, activity declined. Mower Lumber took over in 1942 to cut second-growth logs, but by 1960 they were gone as well, closing the rail operation and the mill.

A group of railfans and local businessmen decided that the railroad should be saved. They approached the state and, after overcoming some initial resistance, a 1961 appropriation created a new state park. Initially the park consisted of the eleven miles of track now in use, three Shays and a host of related equipment. Since that time, the roadbed and quite a few structures in Cass have been rebuilt, the Shays have been reconditioned, and three more Shays plus a Heisler and a Climax have been added to the roster.

The ride is a delight: up eleven miles to the peak of Bald Knob though two switchbacks and up grades as steep as eleven percent. A stop is made at a place called Whittaker where there is a re-creation of a logging camp including some additional rail equipment and a huge Lidgerwood tower skidder that originally brought logs out of the forest on an overhead steel cable.

For those interested in geared steam, the Cass Scenic Railroad is the center of the universe. The equipment is diverse and the state of preservation is high. The opportunity to see everything in motion simply should not be missed.

Georgetown Loop Railroad, Georgetown, CO

1106 Rose St
Georgetown, CO 80444
303-569-2184
www.georgetownlooprr.com

Length	Gauge	Usual Power
3 miles	36 inch	Steam/Diesel

The city of Georgetown, Colorado is at altitude 8,530 feet. Less than two miles further up the canyon is Silver Plume at altitude 9,101, which is five hundred seventy-one feet higher. This presented a huge problem to the 1877 builders of the nar-

Georgetown Loop's number 9, a two-truck Lima Shay, is laid up for minor repairs in front of the engine house.

row gauge Georgetown, Breckenridge, and Leadville Railroad. Silver and gold mines abounded as high as 13,000 feet and there was money to be made in moving the ore from the mines to the smelters. Yet even if a railroad could be built in a straight line between the two towns (it couldn't), the grade would have been prohibitive at 6.5%.

The solution was unusual and daring. The railroad curved back over itself on a giant bridge to gain height, then moved up the canyon to another point where a second reverse move could be made, and finally reached Silver Plume. The daring part was the bridge where the railroad crossed itself. The bridge was almost a hundred feet high on an eighteen-degree curve and a 2% grade. It worked.

The railroad ran its last train in 1941, the result of declining metals prices and increasing auto use. Reconstruction began in 1969. Interstate 70 was moved to avoid the property and in 1984 a replacement bridge was completed, finishing the line between Georgetown and Silver Plume and allowing tourist operations to begin.

Although the Georgetown Loop Railroad is not a museum of antique equipment – there are only a few cars on the property other than the ones in regular service – the ride is exhilarating and well worth while whether behind the number 9 Shay or diesel number 1203, a 1940 Porter.

Durango & Silverton Narrow Gauge Railroad, Durango, CO

479 Main Ave
Durango, CO 81031
970-247-2733
www.durangotrain.com

Length	Gauge	Usual Power
45 miles	36 inch	Steam

In 1871 and 1872 the Denver & Rio Grande built a narrow gauge line south from Denver to Pueblo, Colorado. In succeeding years the line was extended further to El Moro and then west through La Veta Pass to Alamosa. Reaching Antonito, it paralleled the Colorado/New Mexico border to Durango and then turned north to the mining town of Silverton, arriving in 1882. By the late 1880s it had become obvious that the decision to build a narrow gauge line had been a mistake, but it was too late to change.

Durango & Silverton train getting under way from Durango behind locomotive 473, a 1923 Alco 2-8-2.

Initially the Durango-Silverton line survived on freight with passenger service carrying primarily mine workers and other local residents. As the decades passed, however, the freight business was taken over by trucks and the railroad's employees noticed a new passenger business in the form of tourists. In 1961 the Interstate Commerce Commission agreed that the company could suspend winter operations and concentrate on tourism. Then, in 1969, the D&GR finally obtained permission to abandon its tracks south of Durango. The line from Durango to Silverton was sold to a newly formed company, the Durango & Silverton Railroad, and the restoration process began.

The Durango & Silverton doesn't qualify as a railroad museum for the purposes of this book because so little equipment is on display. Escorted yard tours are offered at reasonable prices and there is a small museum in Durango where a few unrestored locomotives can be seen. But the real attraction is one of the greatest train rides anywhere from Durango to Silverton, Colorado along the Animas River behind steam locomotives original to the line. Limited service is provided even in winter and, in most instances, platform and vestibule riding are allowed, giving the railfan a marvelous view of the tracks, the bridges, the scenery and the locomotive ahead.

Cumbres & Toltec Scenic Railroad, Chama, NM

500 Terrace Ave
Chama, NM 87520
719-376-5483
www.cumbrestoltec.com

Length	Gauge	Usual Power
63 miles	36 inch	Steam

The Cumbres &
Toltec is not only a
great ride, but is
also a great muse-
um, described in
detail on page 42.

As the Denver &
Rio Grande closed
down its narrow
gauge operations
(see the Durango &
Silverton descrip-
tion starting on
page 139), a second

Chama yard is almost a hundred percent original to the railroad. A walk through it adds a lot to the incredible ride.

and even longer section of the line was saved from the disman-
tlers. Again the driving force was tourism.

The Denver & Rio Grande obtained permission to abandon the
line from the Interstate Commerce Commission in 1969.
Preservationists, historians and railfans reacted and soon obtained legislative help. In 1970 the states of Colorado and New
Mexico, working together, purchase the line between Antonito
and Chama together with the Chama yard and maintenance facilities, nine steam locomotives and more than a hundred thirty
cars. In 1974 the two states were authorized by the US Congress to create the Cumbres & Toltec Scenic Railroad Commission, a bi-state agency which continues to own and supervise
operation of the road. A volunteer organization, the Friends of
the Cumbres & Toltec, provides care for the historic equipment
and provides interpretation for the public. Operations personnel
are professionals, employed by a contractor.

Other than the yard and the equipment on display (which is discussed on page 42), the important attraction at the Cumbres & Toltec is the ride, an incredible sixty-three miles long. The ride, behind steam, climbs first from 7,800 feet to Cumbres Pass at 10,000 feet then crosses Cascade Creek Trestle and reaches Osier, where a stop is made to serve lunch and water the locomotive. Leaving Osier, the train clings to rock walls and passes through two tunnels before the terrain smooths out. A stop for water is made in Sublette and Antonito is reached after some six hours on the road. Most return to their starting point by bus but for those willing to spend a night, return by rail is possible.

Virginia & Truckee Railroad, Carson City, NV

Eastgate Siding Road
Carson City, NV 89701
775-847-0380
www.virginiatruckee.com

Length	Gauge	Usual Power
11 miles	Standard	Steam

The Virginia & Truckee Railroad crosses some of the richest mining country ever found anywhere. Fantastic sums in gold and silver were taken from the area late in the nineteenth century and early in the twentieth, founding some of the nation's great fortunes. All this was enabled by the Virginia & Truckee, which carried ore to reduction plants, and bullion to the banks and mints of the world.

Business declined as mineral deposits played out. The Virginia & Truckee was closed and abandoned in 1950. Its tracks were pulled up, tunnels dynamited, and equipment sold. Today original V&T cars and locomotives can be found in a number of museums, but not on the railroad.

In 1970 a group of private individuals began to rebuild the railroad, mostly using the original grade. Now standard gauge, it extends (almost) twenty-one miles from Carson City to Virginia City and is operated as a tourist line. Several locomotives are on the railroad, but the primary active steam power is McCloud River RR number 18 (built

McCloud River RR number 18 leads three period passenger cars up the hill to Virginia City through fabulous mining country.

1914), a 2-8-2 Mikado. It pulls a string of ex-DL&W cars which are appropriate for the period, but not original to the road. Originality notwithstanding, the ride is fun, the scenery great, and the history fascinating. Although the V&T doesn't advertise it, well-behaved railfans are sometimes quietly allowed to ride in the vestibules or on the rear platform.

White Pass & Yukon Railway, Skagway, AK

231 Second Avenue
Skagway, AK 99840
800-343-7373
www.whitepassrailroad.com

Length	Gauge	Usual Power
20 miles	36 inch	Diesel

The White Pass & Yukon Railway extends from Skagway, Alaska on the Pacific Ocean at the north end of the famous inland passage, north over the mountains and into Canada. Originally built to reach Whitehorse, Yukon Territory, 110 miles from

Skagway, the road now operates only as far as Carcross, sixty-two miles from Skagway, although the track still exists the rest of the way into Whitehorse. (Most excursion trips only go to White Pass Summit, covering the most scenic 20 miles and stopping short of the international border.)

WP&Y shovelnose diesel number 98 leads Alco number 110 and another shovelnose in a runaround move at White Pass Summit in 2008.

The WP&Y was, of course, originally steam operated and steam locomotives 69 and 73 continue to make the run but, starting in 1954, the railroad purchased eleven of its 90-class shovel-nose diesels and these locomotives have become the line's signature. Interestingly, as originally designed, the shovel-nose itself was intended not for streamling purposes, but instead to actually plow snow. A separate smaller plow was bolted under the nose and flangeway cutting knives were positioned on the lead truck.

Today the 90-class diesels are joined by a fleet of eight Alco hood units that have been on the railroad since the late 1960s and early 1970s as well as more than eighty passenger cars and more than a hundred freight and non-revenue cars. Of the passenger cars, eighteen have nineteenth-century build dates, another eight were built before World War II and the rest are newer, but built with open platforms in the style of the oldest ones.

The White Pass & Yukon climbs from sea level at Skagway to 2,865 feet at White Pass Summit. On the way it clings in places to the side of sheer cliffs, crosses two rivers on high bridges and passes through two tunnels. The bridge at mile 14 is new, having replaced an older steel trestle in 1969, but the original trestle is still there and is easily seen from the train. The scenery is incredible and whether one travels behind steam or vintage diesels, it's a fantastic narrow gauge train ride.

Some Significant Preservation

In addition to the great, the good, the really good and the really great railroad museums, it makes sense to document a few instances of highly significant individual pieces of equipment housed in museums that otherwise wouldn't meet the criteria for inclusion in this book. It also makes sense to document a few equally significant railroad-related sites that have been preserved or are in the process of preservation. If you haven't seen these, they're worth a visit.

Grand Central Terminal

89 E 42nd Street
New York, NY 10017
(212) 340-2583
www.grandcentralterminal.com

Grand Central Terminal (often incorrectly called Grand Central Station) was opened in 1913 as the replacement for an older station that had simply become inadequate to handle the crowds that rode on the New York & Harlem and the New York Central & Hudson River Railroads into and out of New York City. It is a bi-level stub-end station with an underground loop track. Grand Central is said to be the largest passenger station in the world with sixty-seven tracks arranged around forty-four platforms.

145

The main concourse (pictured) is the defining image of Grand Central Terminal. Its famous ceiling depicts a nighttime sky; in the center is the equally famous round information booth topped by a spherical clock. Grand Central was heavily restored between 1994 and 2000 and today it appears much as it did in its early years, although the advertising that dominated the concourse in post-war years is now gone.

Horseshoe Curve

Burgoon Road
Altoona, PA 16601
814.946.0834
www.railroadcity.com

The public facilities at Horseshoe Curve are operated by the Railroaders' Memorial Museum of Altoona; the telephone number and web address shown above are the museum's.

Horseshoe Curve was completed in 1854 as part of the initial construction of the Pennsylvania Railroad between Philadelphia and Pittsburgh. It was made necessary by the grade required to reach Gallitzin, a town only nine miles west-southwest of Altoona as the crow flies, but over nine hundred feet higher. By lengthening the line, the track could climb more gradually, making the route possible.

Horseshoe Curve quickly became a major transportation artery and was shortly four-tracked. During World War II, it handled so much wartime traffic that Nazi Germany even planned to sabotage it (along with other targets) in operation Pastorius.

But two of the saboteur agents, when landed on US soil, immediately defected and the entire plan was aborted.

Horseshoe Curve, now reduced to three tracks, remains a high-volume rail route and has been designated a National Historic Landmark. In its center is a park that includes a visitor center and a 288-foot funicular to raise people from the level of the parking lot to the level of the tracks. Train frequency remains high and the site is well worth a visit.

Allegheny Portage Railroad National Historic Site

110 Federal Park Road
Gallitzin, PA 16641
814-886-6150
www.nps.gov/alpo

In 1826 the Commonwealth of Pennsylvania began the construction of a system of canals between Philadelphia and Pittsburgh. To surmount the Allegheny Mountains a series of ten inclined planes were constructed and each was equipped with rails. Canal boats were floated onto submerged rail cars and then hoisted up the mountain to the next segment of canal by stationary engines at the top of each incline. While no locomotives were used, the inclines do qualify as railroads because they used cars running on fixed rails.

The Portage Railroad opened for business in 1934, but the Pennsylvania Railroad, running the entire distance on rails alone, was completed in 1857 and the canals were quickly made obsolete.

The original equipment from this almost-two-hundred year old railroad is mostly gone, but the National Park Service has preserved engine house number 6 and has recreated some of the equipment it contained. In addition, five miles away, near the town of Mineral Point, one can walk to and through Staple Bend Tunnel, which was dug for the Portage Railroad in 1833 and is considered the oldest railroad tunnel in the country.

Baldwin 60000

The Franklin Institute
222 North 20th Street
Philadelphia, PA 19103
(215) 448-1200
www2.fi.edu

Baldwin number 60000 is an experimental steam locomotive, designed and built by the Baldwin Locomotive Works to test out new ideas. It was a thoroughly modern locomotive (in its day), a three-cylinder compound, and it carried a very unusual water-tube boiler. Designed for dual passenger/freight service, it had sixty-four inch drivers and an estimated top speed of 70 mph.

In tests, the 60000's water tubes proved leaky and its 4-10-2 wheel configuration limited the degree of curvature it could handle. These problems, together with the extra costs involved in maintaining compound locomotives, were problematic to the railroads.

Baldwin attempted to sell the locomotive, but failed and ultimately it went to the Franklin Institute for $1.00 in 1933. It now moves back and forth on fifteen feet of track, powered by hidden hydraulics.

People's Railway number 3, the Shamokin

The Franklin Institute
222 North 20th Street
Philadelphia, PA 19103
(215) 448-1200
www2.fi.edu

Of uncertain ancestry, People's Railway number 3 was probably built in 1842 by Eastwick & Harrison for the Philadelphia & Reading Railroad. In 1873 it was sold to the People's Railway of Pottsville, Pennsylvania.

The People's Railway had begun operations between Pottsville and Minersville, a total of 4.4 miles in central Pennsylvania, in 1871, initially using horses for motive power. The Shamokin replaced at least some of the horses two years later and, still later, overhead wires were strung and electric operations were added. In 1924 the People's Railway was bought by the Reading, which interchanged with it

149

in Pottsville and the Reading thus ended up owning the Shamokin – then eighty-two years old – a second time. Finding little
use for the tiny 4-4-0 locomotive, the Reading donated it to the
Franklin Institute in 1933 and it has been there ever since.

The Rocket

The Franklin Institute
222 North 20th Street
Philadelphia, PA 19103
(215) 448-1200
www2.fi.edu

There were several
locomotives named
"The Rocket" in early
railroad history. The
most famous, an 0-
2-2 by John Ste-
phenson, was the
only successful en-
trant in the Rainhill
Trials of 1829. It
now rests in the Sci-
ence Museum in
London, England.

The Rocket of concern in this book, however, is an inside connected 0-4-0. It was built in London by Braithwaite, Milner &
Co and arrived in the United States in 1838. It was first used
early in 1841 at the opening of the Philadelphia & Reading line
between Reading and Pottsville, Pennsylvania, that line being
the first extension to the original P&R line into Philadelphia.

The Philadelphia & Reading ran down the Schuylkill Valley almost all the way between Reading and Philadelphia. First built
as a double-track line, it was the first railroad in the US to be
double-tracked and thus the Rocket one of the first engines to
run at speed past another locomotive, also at speed.

In active service for over forty years, The Rocket was displayed
at the World's Columbian Exposition in 1893 and again at the
St. Louis Exposition in 1904. It was donated to the Franklin
Institute in 1933.

Washington Union Station

50 Massachusetts Avenue NE
Washington, DC 20002
(202) 289-1908
www.unionstationdc.com

Washington Union
Station was built
by the Pennsylva-
nia and Baltimore
& Ohio railroads,
first opening in
1907 and com-
pleted in 1908.
The Southern
Railway and the
Richmond, Freder-
icksburg & Poto-
mac later built in-
to the station;
connections with
the Atlantic Coast Line and Seaboard Railways were provided
via trackage rights.

Like Grand Central Terminal in New York, Washington Union
Station has tracks on two levels, but unlike Grand Central,
some tracks terminate and others pass through the station pro-
ceeding underground to the south. Trains from the north, south
and west can thus all be accommodated.

Famously, in 1953, Pennsylvania Railroad GG1 number 4876
pulling The Federal, lost its brakes two miles out from the sta-

tion. The locomotive destroyed the stationmaster's office and almost made its way into the concourse before the floor gave out, dropping 4876 into the station basement. Warnings had been radioed ahead, so there were injuries, but no deaths as a result. Number 4876 was later hauled out, repaired, and put back in service.

By 1980 Union Station was in serious decline and had become an embarrassment to the nation's capital. It was rebuilt and restored with the work completed in 1988. Today it serves Amtrak, the MARC and VRE commuter railways, and the Washington Metro Red Line.

The John Bull

Smithsonian Institution
National Museum of American History
12th St. and Constitution Ave
Washington, DC 20013
(202) 633-1000
americanhistory.si.edu

The John Bull is one of the oldest loco-motives in existence. It was built in England in 1831 and imported into the United States for service on the Camden & Amboy Railroad, the first railroad chartered in the United States (but not the first built). The line ran from Camden, New Jersey just across the Delaware River from Philadelphia, north to Amboy (now Perth Amboy) just across the Arthur Kill from Staten Island and thus only a short boat ride from New York City.

The Camden & Amboy, including the John Bull, was purchased by the Pennsylvania Railroad in 1871 and the John Bull was stored, being fired up in 1876 and again in 1883 for expositions. The locomotive was purchased from the Pennsylvania by the Smithsonian Institution in 1884 and became one of the museum's first industrial artifacts. In 1981 the John Bull reached the age of a hundred-fifty and, in celebration, the Smithsonian briefly operated it under its own power. It remains in technically operable condition but is unlikely to see steam again anytime soon.

Martinsburg B&O Roundhouse

100 E Liberty St
Martinsburg, WV 25404
(304) 260-4141
www.martinsburgroundhouse.com

In 1866, following the US Civil War, the Baltimore & Ohio Railroad rebuilt the Martinsburg, West Virginia shops that had been destroyed during the war. The buildings were then used by the railroad on a continuing basis for more than a hundred years.

The great railroad strike of 1877 started on July 14 in Martinsburg and soon spread throughout the east and Midwest. Federal troops were used to quell violence and the strike came to an end after a month and a half of paralysis for the railroads.

In 1988 the last work was moved elsewhere and the shop complex sat vacant. In 1990 vandals set fire to the east roundhouse, destroying it. (There had been two roundhouses; the east one was the newer.) In 2000 Berkeley County purchased the shop complex and renovation and restoration began.

As this is written, the B&O Martinsburg shops and the 1866 roundhouse are not open to visitors, but it is hoped that they will be soon and, even if they aren't, they remain an important and interesting instance of preservation.

The General

Southern Museum of Civil War and Locomotive History
2829 Cherokee St
Kennesaw, GA 30144
(770) 427-2117
www.southernmuseum.org

The General is an American 4-4-0 built in 1855 by Rogers, Ketchum & Grosvenor in Paterson, New Jersey for the Western & Atlantic Railroad. It was stolen from its regular train crew by James Andrews and a group of Union men while the crew and passengers were eating breakfast in Big Shanty, Georgia. The resulting epic "Great Locomotive Chase" that ultimately ended in Andrews' capture, trial and execution has been the subject of numerous movies and books and is justly famous.

The Southern Museum of Civil War and Locomotive History is a smallish museum with The General itself as the star attraction. But despite its size, the museum does have other things of interest:

- Several nicely done displays about the Civil War and wartime railroading including the Andrews Raid
- The Glover Machine Works, a restored and relocated locomotive manufacturing shop dating from the post-war reconstruction area and featuring two restored locomotives undergoing assembly
- The "Merci Train" car given by the French people to the state of Georgia following World War II.

Cincinnati Union Station

1301 Western Ave
Cincinnati, OH 45203
(513) 287-7000
www.cincymuseum.org

Cincinnati Union Station was built by the Big Four, Pennsylvania, Chesapeake & Ohio, Norfolk & Western, Southern, Louisville & Nashville, and Baltimore & Ohio railroads to replace outmoded and inefficient earlier stations. Completed in 1933 it soon became famous for its art deco design and for the gorgeous mosaics that decorated its interior in a celebration of Cincinnati industry.

Although the station saw heavy use during World War II, it quickly became an outsized white elephant after the war. After Amtrak took over the nation's passenger service in 1971, the concourse was torn down, Amtrak moved out, and the headhouse fell into disrepair. (The mosaics, thankfully, were saved and can be seen today at the Cincinnati airport.) In the 1980s an attempt to use the building as a shopping center failed and it again stood vacant. Then, in 1990, work began on its conversion into a Museum Center. That work has been successful and the headhouse has been restored to something approaching its former grace – a sight well worth seeing.

And – for the true railfan – the Cincinnati Railroad Club occupies the former Tower A, high atop the terminal with an excellent view of the still-active freight yard. The public is invited to visit and watch the action as trains come and go.

The Reuben Wells

Children's Museum of Indianapolis
3000 N Meridian St
Indianapolis, IN 46208
(317) 334-3322
www.childrensmuseum.org

The Reuben Wells is an 0-10-0 steam locomotive that was built in 1868 by and for the Jeffersonville, Madison & Indianapolis Railroad. At the time of its completion it was the most powerful steam locomotive in the world,

designed to lift cars up the steep 6% two-mile long incline from the Ohio River to level ground at Madison, Indiana. The "incline" was and still is the steepest mainline grade in the US; in the nineteenth century, cars had to be pushed up because couplers weren't strong enough to allow them to be pulled.

The Reuben Wells worked thirty years in Madison and spent another seven years as backup power before being retired. It was donated first to Purdue University and from there went through several hands before ending up with the Pennsylvania Railroad (by then, the owner of the Madison incline). In 1968 the Pennsylvania donated the Reuben Wells to the Children's Museum where it has been ever since.

Unfortunately the Children's Museum has seen fit to devote only minimal space to the locomotive's display so it is hard to see and hard to photograph. Even then, the Wells is significant enough to make a visit worthwhile.

The Pioneer (4-2-0)

Chicago History Museum
1601 N. Clark St.
Chicago, IL 60614
312.642.4600
www.chicagohs.org

The Pioneer, an unusual 4-2-0 steam locomotive, was built by Baldwin in 1837 for the Utica & Schenectady Railroad and was sold in 1848 to the Galena & Chicago Union where it became the first locomotive to operate in revenue service out of Chicago. It

worked for the G&CU, Chicago's first railroad, and for the Chicago Burlington & Quincy until its retirement in 1874. It was in the Field Museum (of Chicago) from 1894 to 1904 and in the Museum of Science and Industry (also of Chicago) from 1934 to 1947. After a rebuild by the Chicago & Northwestern, it operated at the 1948 Chicago Railroad Fair and was donated to the Chicago History Museum in 1972.

Probably for dramatic effect, the Chicago History Museum has chosen to display The Pioneer under colored lights. It is easy to see and visitors can get close enough to see it in detail, but the lighting makes it very hard to photograph.

The Pioneer Zephyr

Museum of Science & Industry
1 South Lake Shore Drive
Chicago, IL 60637
(773) 684-1414
www.msichicago.org

The Museum of Science and Industry is primarily a children's museum (and an excellent one), but it holds several artifacts of great interest to railfans. Key among them are the Pioneer Zephyr, New York Central locomotive

999, and the Mississippi (see the listings that follow).

The Pioneer Zephyr was built in 1934 by Budd for the Chicago, Burlington & Quincy Railroad. It famously raced non-stop from Denver to Chicago in thirteen hours and five minutes with thousands watching from trackside at every small town along the way as it flashed by. That fall the train entered regular service between Kansas City, Omaha and Lincoln.

The Pioneer Zephyr was retired by the CB&Q in 1960 and was donated to the Museum of Science and Industry where it has been on display ever since. Until 1998 it was stored outside, subject to the weather, but then the museum built an underground display room, restored the train cosmetically and installed it. Today it is both visible and protected for the future.

The Pioneer Zephyr is generally considered the first successful streamlined train in the United States and was also among the first stainless-steel, rib-sided, articulated and unitized ones.

New York Central number 999

Museum of Science & Industry
1 South Lake Shore Drive
Chicago, IL 60637
(773) 684-1414
www.msichicago.org

New York Central's locomotive 999, a 4-4-0 American, was built with eighty-six inch drivers to pull the Empire State Express. It was said to have reached a top speed of 112 mph on May 10, 1893 in an exhibition run and became famous for that legend, which the New York Central never confirmed (but never denied, either).

159

The 999's eighty-six inch drivers were replaced with seventy-inch ones during the locomotive's service life, most likely because super high speed was no long as important as pulling power. The replacement is a pity because it removes some of the uniqueness of the locomotive, but its essence remains unchanged.

As time passed, the 999's design became obsolete. It was shown at numerous expositions including the Chicago Railroad Fair and then retired from service in 1952. The New York Central donated the 999 to the Museum of Science and Industry in 1962 where it was displayed outside through 1998. Then, after a cosmetic rejuvenation, it was moved indoors where it remains.

The Mississippi

Museum of Science & Industry
1 South Lake Shore Drive
Chicago, IL 60637
(773) 684-1414
www.msichicago.org

The Mississippi, although little known, is one of the oldest preserved steam locomotives in the world. It was built circa 1834, probably by Braithwaite, Milner & Co of England and assembled that same year probably by Dunham & Co of New York. It served  on several small railroads in the Vicksburg area and for the Confederacy during the Civil War. After traveling under its own power to Chicago to be displayed at the 1893 World's Columbian

Exposition, it was placed in Chicago's Field Museum and in 1927 was transferred to the Rosenwald Industrial Museum (which later became the Museum of Science and Industry). The history of The Mississippi is somewhat clouded but, if the dates are correct, in the USA, only the John Bull is older.

It should also be noted that the Museum of Science and Industry has several other ancient steam locomotives. Although reproductions, they are themselves old enough to be of great interest: The John Stevens (original built 1825, replica built 1928 by the Pennsylvania Railroad), The Rocket (original built 1829 by George and Robert Stevenson, replica built 1931 by Robert Stevenson & Co) and The York (original built 1831 by Phineas Davis, replica built 1927 by the Baltimore & Ohio Railroad).

Kansas City Union Station

30 West Pershing Road
Kansas City, MO 64108
(816) 460-2020
www.unionstation.org

Kansas City's Union Station is one of the less-known great granite halls of transportation of the early twentieth century. It was built in 1914 by the Kansas City Terminal Railway, a cooperative venture owned by the  twelve railroads that served the city. Located in a valley that leads toward the Mississippi River, it is on a natural incline that assists trains moving from or to the river crossing. T-shaped, the building has a grand hall with a ninety-five foot ceiling and a

waiting room/ concourse that originally extended over the
tracks. The tracks under the concourse are now gone, but the
concourse itself remains.

Passenger volume fell dramatically after World War II; Amtrak
took over the nation's passenger services in 1971 and moved out
of KC Union Station in 1985. Standing vacant, the building began to decay. A public/private non-profit coalition began reconstruction of the station in 1997, completing it in 1999. Amtrak
returned in 2002, joining a number of museums, shops and res-
taurants. (Your author can testify that Pierponts's Restaurant
is excellent.) The grand hall and the concourse are both in good
condition and the building is well worth a visit even if all the visitor does is soak in the atmosphere.

Golden Spike National Historic Site

Promontory, UT 84307
(435) 471-2209
www.nps.gov/gosp

Golden Spike Na-
tional Historic Site
is the place where
the transcon-
tinental railroad
was completed. It
is the place where
the famous golden
spike was driven,
joining the Central
Pacific and the Un-
ion Pacific rail-
roads. No longer
served by rail, the site is now federally owned and operated by
the US National Park Service. It is an isolated spot in the de-
sert, but one worth visiting.

Arriving at the site one finds a visitor center and a small museum containing some artifacts of the period, but no actual nineteenth century rolling stock. Instead, and almost as good, the Park Service has built two steam locomotives closely duplicating the Union Pacific 119 and the Central Pacific *Jupiter*, the locomotives that actually were present at the spike driving ceremony. It has also laid about a half-mile of track, installed a turning wye, and built at a discreet distance an engine house for storing the locomotives. From time to time re-enactments are performed.

The Park Service has also preserved some of the original roadbed. Graveled, not paved, it is open to automobiles and the visitor can see actual earthworks thrown up by Central Pacific and Union Pacific grading crews.

Los Angeles Union Passenger Terminal

800 N Alameda St
Los Angeles, CA
(800) 872-7245
en.wikipedia.org/wiki/Union_Station_(Los_Angeles)

Los Angeles Union Passenger Terminal (now known as Los Angeles Union Station) first opened to the public in July 1939. Unlike most other big-city passenger stations, it is not a granite monolith, but instead has a distinctive southwest aura both in its architecture and in the gardens that go with it. Its design is a combination of Spanish Colonial, Mission Revival and Art Deco (or Streamline Moderne) elements.

LAUPT originally served the Atchison, Topeka & Santa Fe Railway, the Southern Pacific Railroad, and the Union Pacific Railroad, as well as the Pacific Electric Railway and the Los Angeles Railway. Today is remains in heavy use by Amtrak, Metrolink, Metro Rail and a host of bus services. Many interior spaces and the exterior of the terminal remain essentially unchanged from its opening day.

Indexes, Acknowledgements and Credits

Museums by Name

Museums by State

Special Artifact Index and Some Facts

As mentioned in the introduction, the sixty-seven museums covered in this book hold a total of more than five thousand locomotives and cars and occupy a little more than two square miles of land. Since the great majority of the museums are volunteer, non-profit organizations, there is a good deal of variation between them. Not all research their holdings or maintain detailed records but, to the extent that data is available, a few facts might be of interest.

Based on equipment counts from the museum's rosters, the most-preserved railroad is the Denver & Rio Grande (and the D&RGW), mostly due to the huge amount of equipment preserved by the Cumbres & Toltec and the Colorado Railroad Museum. Second most-preserved is the Pennsylvania, closely followed by the Southern Pacific, the Southern, the Western Pacific, the Santa Fe and the Union Pacific. These roads are heavily represented, of course, in part to their size, but also due to their own internal sense of history and to the number of railfans and enthusiasts encouraging the preservation of their equipment.

The most-preserved electric railroads are the Massachusetts Bay Area Transportation Authority and the Chicago Transit Authority with the Pacific Electric solidly in third place. For industrial and private lines, Rayonier and Pickering Lumber top the list.

The most often preserved steam locomotive is the 2-8-0 Consolidation, closely followed by the 2-8-2 Mikado, the 0-4-0, and the 0-6-0. Among EMD diesels, the most commonly preserved unit is the heavy switcher (defined as anything in excess of forty-four tons); the next most common group is the light switcher followed by the F-unit in all its variations and the GP and its variations.

The most preserved passenger car type is the coach; coaches make up almost half the museums' fleets. In freight, the common boxcar and the caboose are most popular with flatcars a distant third. Among non-revenue equipment, the crane in all its variations and sizes is the most common item.

Among commercial builders, Pullman (and Pullman Standard) outnumbers all others by a factor larger than two. American Car and Foundry is second. EMD (and predecessor EMC) are the most commonly found locomotive builders with Alco, Baldwin and General Electric far behind. Among the railroads that built cars and locomotives, the Pennsylvania is by far the best represented builder in the museums' fleets.

For the dedicated railfan, the museums listed in this book hold many fascinating and unique pieces. The index below lists those specific items that your author finds unique (or at least unusual) and fascinating. The reader should be aware that not all of these items will be accessible to visitors at all times and not all of them have been restored.

Type	Item	Museum
Steam Locomotives		
0-4-0	Camden & Amboy John Bull (1831)	Smithsonian Institution
0-4-0	Baltimore & Ohio 2 Atlantic (Baltimore & Ohio 1832)	B&O Railroad Museum
0-4-0	Unknown Mississippi (Braithwaite, Milner & Co 1834)	Museum of Science and Industry
0-4-0	Baltimore & Ohio 8 John Hancock (Baltimore & Ohio 1836)	B&O Railroad Museum
4-2-0	Galena & Chicago Union Pioneer (Baldwin Locomotive Works 1837)	Chicago History Museum
0-4-0	Philadelphia & Reading Rocket (Braithwaite, Milner & Co 1838)	Franklin Institute
The six oldest locomotives in the USA. B&O number 2 and 8 are grasshopper types.		

Type	Item	Museum
0-4-2T	Manitou & Pike's Peak 1 (Baldwin Locomotive Works 1893)	Colorado Railroad Museum
A cog railway locomotive with a canted boiler		
0-8-0	Baltimore & Ohio 57 Memnon (Newcastle Manufacturing Company 1853)	B&O Railroad Museum
Another ancient locomotive. Has canted cylinders		
0-10-0	Jeffersonville, Madison & Indianapolis Reuben Wells (Jeffersonville, Madison & Indianapolis 1868)	Children's Museum of Indianapolis
The locomotive that proved that railroads could climb hills		
2-2-2T	Reading Railroad Black Diamond (Baldwin Locomotive Works 1889)	St. Louis Museum of Transportation
An inspection engine: a passenger car body mounted over a steam locomotive chassis		
2-6-0	Carson & Tahoe Lumber & Fluming 1 Glenbrook (Baldwin Locomotive Works 1875)	Nevada State Railroad Museum
A very early narrow-gauge Mogul		
2-6-6-2	United States Plywood 11 (Baldwin Locomotive Works 1926)	Northwest Railway Museum
2-6-6-2	Weyerhaeuser Timber Company 6 (Baldwin Locomotive Works 1928)	Northwest Railway Museum
2-6-6-2	Chesapeake & Ohio 1309 (Baldwin Locomotive Works 1949)	B&O Railroad Museum
2-6-6-2T	Weyerhaeuser Timber Company 108 (Baldwin Locomotive Works 1926)	Northwest Railway Museum
2-6-6-2T	California Western 46 (Baldwin Locomotive Works 1937)	Pacific Southwest Railroad Museum
Five interesting logging mallets		
2-6-6-4	Norfolk & Western 1218 (Norfolk & Western 1943)	Virginia Museum of Transportation
Norfolk & Western's A class, a dual-service mallet. Made famous in excursion service in the 1980s and early 1990s		

Great Railroad Museums of the USA
Indexes

Type	Item	Museum
2-6-6-6	Chesapeake & Ohio 1604 (Lima Locomotive Works 1941)	B&O Railroad Museum
A C&O Allegheny		
2-8-0	Denver Leadville & Gunnison 191 (Baldwin Locomotive Works 1880)	Colorado Railroad Museum
In your author's humble opinion, the prettiest steam locomotive existing		
2-8-8-2	Norfolk & Western 2050 (American Locomotive Company 1923)	Illinois Railway Museum
2-8-8-2	Norfolk & Western 2156 (Norfolk & Western 1942)	St. Louis Museum of Transportation
Two examples of the Norfolk & Western Y-class, one of the most successful drag freight locomotives of all time		
2-8-8-4	Duluth Missabe & Iron Range Railway 227 (Baldwin Locomotive Works 1941)	Lake Superior Railroad Museum
The DM&IR Yellowstone was a heavy-duty ore hauler		
4-10-2	Baldwin Locomotive Works 60000 (Baldwin Locomotive Works 1926)	Franklin Institute
Baldwin's 60,000th locomotive. Highly innovative, it was ahead of its time and Baldwin was never able to sell it.		
4-2-4T	Southern Pacific 1 C P Huntington (Cooke Locomotive Works 1863)	California State Railroad Museum
A very early steam locomotive that saw service in the construction of the Central Pacific leg of the transcontinental railroad.		
4-4-0	People's Railway 3 Shamokin (Eastwick & Harrison 1842)	Franklin Institute
A very early American-type and the first locomotive to operate in Chicago.		
4-4-0	Western & Atlantic The General (Rogers, Ketchum & Grosvenor 1855)	Southern Museum of Civil War and Locomotive History
The famous "General" from the "Great Locomotive Chase"		
4-4-0	Baltimore & Ohio 25 William Mason (Mason Machine Works 1856)	B&O Railroad Museum
Another very old 4-4-0 American		

Type	Item	Museum
4-4-0	St. Paul & Pacific 1 William Crooks (Smith & Jackson 1861)	Lake Superior Railroad Museum
A very early steam locomotive by an unusual builder. No other locomotives by Smith & Jackson are known to exist		
4-4-0	Central Pacific 1 Gov. Stanford (Richard Norris 1862)	California State Railroad Museum
A very early steam locomotive by a builder who was instrumental in the early development of the field		
4-4-0	New York Central 999 (New York Central 1893)	Museum of Science and Industry
The 999 reputedly once achieved 112 miles per hour		
4-4-0	Delaware Lackawanna & Western 952 (American Locomotive Company 1905)	St. Louis Museum of Transportation
4-4-2	Central New Jersey 592 (American Locomotive Company 1901)	B&O Railroad Museum
Two anthracite-burning camelbacks, also known as Mother Hubbards		
4-4-2	Pennsylvania Railroad 460 (Pennsylvania Railroad 1914)	Railroad Museum of Pennsylvania
The locomotive that famously beat an airplane rushing film of Lindberg to New York City.		
4-4-4	Canadian Pacific 2929 (Canadian Locomotive Works 1938)	Steamtown National Historic Site
The Canadian Pacific's rare Jubilee class, an unusual wheel arrangement designed for speed in passenger service		
4-6-2	Pennsylvania Railroad 1361 (Pennsylvania Railroad 1918)	Railroaders Memorial Museum
4-6-2	Pennsylvania Railroad 3750 (Pennsylvania Railroad 1920)	Railroad Museum of Pennsylvania
The two surviving examples of the Pennsylvania Railroad's K-class, arguably one of the most successful passenger locomotive designs of all time		
4-6-2	British Railways Board 60008 Dwight D Eisenhower (London Northeaster RR 1937)	National Railroad Museum
A British-designed and built 3-cylinder streamlined Pacific.		

Type	Item	Museum
4-6-4	Chesapeake & Ohio 490 (American Locomotive Company 1920)	B&O Railroad Museum
Chesapeake & Ohio 490 still retains its 1930s streamlining		
4-8-8-2	Southern Pacific 4294 (Baldwin Locomotive Works 1944)	California State Railroad Museum
The only surviving Southern Pacific cab-forward		
4-8-8-4	Union Pacific 4006 (American Locomotive Company 1941)	St. Louis Museum of Transportation
4-8-8-4	Union Pacific 4018 (American Locomotive Company 1941)	Museum of the American Railroad
4-8-8-4	Union Pacific 4012 (American Locomotive Company 1941)	Steamtown National Historic Site
4-8-8-4	Union Pacific 4017 (American Locomotive Company 1941)	National Railroad Museum
Four surviving "big boys." Others exist but these are in museums and can be visited.		
Diesel Locomotives		
132T	Wellsville Addison & Galeton 1700 (General Electric 1940)	Lake Shore Railway Museum
One of three 132-ton diesels built by General Electric originally for the Ford Motor Company and uniquely styled to match the 1938 Ford car.		
Aerotrain	General Motors 2 (Electromotive Di-vision (GM) 1955)	National Railroad Museum
Aerotrain	Chicago Rock Island & Pacific 3 (Electromotive Division (GM) 1955)	St. Louis Museum of Transportation
In 1955 General Motors built three experimental train sets with automotive technology and styling. Two remain, each consisting of a locomotive and two passenger coaches. Unfortunately the unique tail cars have been lost.		
Boxcab	Baltimore & Ohio 1 (Alco/GE/Ingersoll Rand 1925)	St. Louis Museum of Transportation
Boxcab	Central New Jersey 1000 (Alco/GE/Ingersoll Rand 1925)	B&O Railroad Museum
Boxcab	Union Carbide 11 (General Electric/Ingersoll-Rand 1926)	North Alabama Railroad Museum

Type	Item	Museum
Boxcab	Delaware Lackawanna & Western 3001 (Alco/GE/Ingersoll Rand 1926)	Illinois Railway Museum
Boxcab	Foley Brothers Construction 110-1 (General Electric/Ingersoll-Rand 1929)	Western Pacific Railroad Museum
Boxcab	Armco Steel B-70 (Baldwin/Westinghouse 1929)	Southeastern Railway Museum
Boxcab	Baltimore & Ohio 50 (Electro Motive Corporation 1935)	St. Louis Museum of Transportation
Seven very early diesel locomotives. B&O number 50, although a little later in construction, is believed to be the first diesel to enter revenue passenger service.		
DD40AX	Union Pacific 6916 (Electromotive Division (GM) 1969)	Utah State Railroad Museum
DD40AX	Union Pacific 6913 (Electromotive Division (GM) 1969)	Museum of the American Railroad
DD40AX	Union Pacific 6930 (Electromotive Division (GM) 1970)	Illinois Railway Museum
DD40AX	Union Pacific 6944 (Electromotive Division (GM) 1971)	St. Louis Museum of Transportation
DD40AX	Union Pacific 6946 (Electromotive Division (GM) 1971)	Western Pacific Railroad Museum
Five of the Union Pacific's famous "double diesels"		
E3	Atlantic Coast Line 501 (Electromotive Division (GM) 1939)	North Carolina Transportation Museum
A very rare and very early E-unit		
E5	Chicago Burlington & Quincy 9911A (Electromotive Division (GM) 1940)	Illinois Railway Museum
The only surviving E5 diesel and five matching cars, comprising the almost-complete CB&Q Nebraska Zephyr train.		
H24-66	BDL Company 9905 (Fairbanks-Morse)	Reading Railroad Heritage Museum
An engine-less slug made from a Fairbanks-Morse Trainmaster. Although cut down, the outline of the Trainmaster can still be seen in the shape of the slug.		

Type	Item	Museum
PA-1	Atchison Topeka & Santa Fe 59L (American Locomotive Company 1948)	Museum of the American Railroad
The Alco PA-1 is most railfan's favorite diesel. Two units survive in the USA and this one is the only one in a museum. At the time this book was published, it is beginning restoration and will not be publicly available for some years to come.		
Shovel-nose	Chicago Burlington & Quincy Pioneer Zephyr (Budd Manufacturing Company 1934)	Museum of Science and Industry
Shovel-nose	Chicago Burlington & Quincy 9908 Silver Charger (Electro Motive Corporation 1939)	St. Louis Museum of Transportation
Two rib-sided, shovelnose diesels from the 1930s. The Pioneer Zephyr includes its complete train.		
Visibility Cab	Armco Steel B73 (Baldwin/Westinghouse 1930)	Pennsylvania Trolley Museum
Visibility Cab	Armco Steel B71 (Westinghouse 1930)	Minnesota Transportation Museum
Two Visibility Cab locomotives. The visibility cab locomotive had a unique body design giving an interesting appearance. They were the first diesels to separate the cab from the engine compartment. Only eleven were ever built.		
Electric Locomotives		
Bipolar	Chicago Milwaukee St. Paul & Pacific (Milwaukee Road) E-2 (General Electric 1919)	St. Louis Museum of Transportation
Five so-called "bi-polar" locomotives were built by General Electric for the Milwaukee Road's western electrification in 1919. This is the only survivor of that iconic class.		
Boxcab	General Electric 1 (Thompson-Houston 1892)	St. Louis Museum of Transportation
Boxcab	Singer Company 1 (General Electric 1898)	Indiana Transportation Museum
Boxcab	South Brooklyn Railway 4 (1907)	Shore Line Trolley Museum
Three very early electrics. General Electric number 1 is said to have been the first US main line electric locomotive.		

Type	Item	Museum
DD-1	Pennsylvania Railroad 3936 and 3937 (Pennsylvania Railroad 1911)	Railroad Museum of Pennsylvania
The Pennsylvania Railroad's DD-1 locomotives operated in pairs, serving New York City between Sunnyside Yard and Manhattan Transfer.		
EL-C	Virginian 135 (General Electric 1956)	Virginia Museum of Transportation
A dozen EL-C locomotives were built for the Virginian by General Electric in 1956 as replacements for aging boxcab motors. This one survives following service both on the Virginian and the New York, New Haven & Hartford.		
Little Joe	Chicago South Shore & South Bend 802 (General Electric 1949)	Lake Shore Railway Museum
Little Joe	Chicago South Shore & South Bend 803 (General Electric 1949)	Illinois Railway Museum
The "Little Joes" were built for service in Russia but diverted by the Cold War		
S motor	Penn Central Railroad 4715 (Alco/GE 1906)	Illinois Railway Museum
S motor	New York Central 113 (Alco/GE 1906)	St. Louis Museum of Transportation
Iconic electric locomotives that served for more than fifty years in New York's Grand Central Terminal		
Steeple cab	Derby Horse Railway Derby (1888)	Shore Line Trolley Museum
Steeple cab	Ponemaugh Mills 1386 (General Electric 1894)	Connecticut Trolley Museum
Steeple cab	Key System 1215 (Key System 1899)	Western Railway Museum
Three ancient steeplecab locomotives. The "Derby" is likely the oldest electric locomotive in the USA.		
Other Power		
Boxcab	Dan Patch Lines 100 (General Electric 1913)	Minnesota Transportation Museum
Dan Patch Lines number 100 was originally built in 1913 as a gas-electric power car. It was later converted to electric operation and still later converted to run as a diesel		

Type	Item	Museum
Mule	Erie Dock Company 7 (Atlas Car Company 1910)	Lake Shore Railway Museum
Mule	Panama Canal 686 (General Electric 1914)	Virginia Museum of Transportation
Mule	Panama Canal 662 (General Electric 1914)	St. Louis Museum of Transportation
Mule	Pennsylvania Power & Light 2 (Atlas Car Company 1920)	Mad River & NKP Museum
As we have used the term, a "mule' is an electrically-driven locomotive that runs on its own set of narrow-gauge tracks and drags behind it loads on adjacent tracks or, in some cases, ships in a canal. While not traditional railroading, they are unusual and interesting to see and they do run on rails.		
McKeen Cars	Chicago Great Western 1000 and Virginia & Truckee 22 (McKeen Motor Car Company 1910)	Nevada State Railroad Museum
Two McKeen cars survive. CGW 1000 is operational but, unfortunately, V&T 22 serves as a parts donor and is little more than scrap.		
Doodle-bug	San Luis Valley Railroad M-300 (1924)	Oklahoma Railroad Museum
Doodle-bug	Tucson, Cornelia & Gila Bend 401 (Edwards Railway Motor Car Co 1926)	Nevada State Railroad Museum
Doodle-bug	East Broad Top M-1 (East Broad Top RR 1927)	East Broad Top Railroad
Doodle-bug	Atchison Topeka & Santa Fe M160 (J G Brill Car Company 1931)	Museum of the American Railroad
Doodlebugs are fascinating creatures, varying all the way from home-built collections of junk to semi-streamlined power units. Santa Fe M160 wears warbonnet paint.		
Goose	Rio Grande Southern 2 (Rio Grande Southern 1931)	Colorado Railroad Museum
Goose	Rio Grande Southern 6 (Rio Grande Southern 1934)	Colorado Railroad Museum
Goose	Rio Grande Southern 7 (Rio Grande Southern 1936)	Colorado Railroad Museum
Six of the original seven Rio Grande Southern "geese" survive. These three are at the Colorado Railroad Museum		

Type	Item	Museum
Experi-mental	US Department of Transporta-tion Garrett, TLRV and Rohr	Pueblo Railway Museum
These three units were built for experimental purposes and were test-ed at the Department of Transportation's test site near Pueblo, Colo-rado. They represent a fascinating look at what "might have been."		
Turbine	Union Pacific 18 (General Elec-tric 1960)	Illinois Railway Museum
Turbine	Union Pacific 26 (General Elec-tric 1961)	Utah State Railroad Mu-seum
Fifty-two of the fifty-four Union Pacific gas turbines have been scrapped, but these two were preserved. Massive, hugely powerful and (for a time) quite successful, they are worth a visit to see.		
Passenger Cars		
Coach	Boston & Providence None (Boston & Providence 1833)	St. Louis Museum of Transportation
Coach	Baltimore & Ohio Maryland and Ohio (Richard Imlay, 1830)	B&O Railroad Museum
Extremely early "stagecoach" passenger cars with the body suspended on straps over 4-wheel chasses.		
Coach	Camden & Amboy 3 (Camden & Amboy 1836)	Railroad Museum of Pennsylvania
Coach	General Mining Association of Nova Scotia (Timothy Hack-worth 1838)	B&O Railroad Museum 4-wheel
Coach	Central New Jersey 21 (Wason Manufacturing Company 1868)	B&O Railroad Museum
Coach	Virginia & Truckee 17 (Central Pacific 1868)	Nevada State Railroad Museum
Coach	Central Pacific 43 (Wason Manufacturing Company 1869)	Railtown 1897 State His-toric Park
Coach	Virginia & Truckee 3, 4, 9, and 10 (Kimball Carriage & Car Mfg. Co. 1872 and 1873)	Nevada State Railroad Museum
Coach	Virginia & Truckee 11 and 12 (J G Brill Car Company 1874)	Nevada State Railroad Museum
A selection of very early passenger equipment.		
Coach	Southern Pacific 2445 and 2446 (Pullman and Pull-man/Standard 1941)	Orange Empire Railroad Museum
Southern Pacific's articulated coaches (two cars on three trucks)		

Type	Item	Museum
Coach	Hartsfield International Airport 1 and 53 (Westinghouse 1980)	Southeastern Railway Museum
Fully-automated underground rail cars from the Atlanta airport where they shuttled passengers between terminals until 2002		
Combine	Cumberland Valley B (Cumberland Valley RR 1855)	Railroad Museum of Pennsylvania
Combine	East Jordan & Southern 2 (Osgood Bradley Car Company 1864)	Mid-Continent Railway Museum
Combine	Virginia & Truckee 8 Julia Bulette (Virginia & Truckee 1869)	Nevada State Railroad Museum
Combine	Monterey & Salinas Valley 1 (Carter Brothers 1874)	California State Railroad Museum
Combine	Virginia & Truckee 15 and 16 (Detroit Car Works 1874)	California State Railroad Museum
Combine	Eureka & Palisade 3 (Billmeyer & Smalls 1874)	Nevada State Railroad Museum
Express	Virginia & Truckee 14 (Oxford Cooperative Car Co. 1874)	Nevada State Railroad Museum
A selection of early post-Civil War combines. Cumberland Valley combine B has an outside corridor past the baggage section. Virginia & Truckee number 8 was named after Nevada's most famous courtesan and madam, Julia Bulette.		
Private	Georgia Northern 100 Gold Coast (Central of Georgia 1905)	California State Railroad Museum
Lucius Beebe's first private car		
Private	Pullman Ferdinand Magellan (Pullman 1928)	Gold Coast Railroad Museum
A private car built by Pullman in 1928. Armor-plated, it was used by several US Presidents		
Private	Wisconsin Fish Commission 2 Badger (Pullman 1913)	Mid-Continent Railway Museum
Private	J G Shedd Aquarium Nautilus (Thrall Manufacturing Company 1957)	Monticello Railway Museum
Two unusual private cars. The Wisconsin car was built to carry fish between hatcheries and lakes and rivers; the Shedd car moved fish in the other direction: from where they were caught to the aquarium.		

Type	Item	Museum
Freight Cars		
Boxcar	Singer Company 132 and 145 (1869)	Connecticut Trolley Museum
Two ancient boxcars; the oldest known freight equipment in the USA		
Boxcar	Virginia & Truckee 1005 (Central Pacific 1872)	Nevada State Railroad Museum
Boxcar	Virginia & Truckee 1011 and 1013 (Wells & French 1874)	Nevada State Railroad Museum
Three very old boxcars. Number 1005 is a 28-footer		
Boxcar	Baltimore & Ohio 376321 (Baltimore & Ohio 1910)	B&O Railroad Museum
Boxcar	Baltimore & Ohio 174065 (Baltimore & Ohio 1925)	Illinois Railway Museum
Two of the Baltimore & Ohio's iconic wagon-top boxcars		
Boxcar	Chicago Milwaukee St. Paul & Pacific 19331 (Chicago Milwaukee St. Paul & Pacific 1940)	Illinois Railway Museum
A Milwaukee Road rib-sided boxcar		
Boxcar	McCloud River Railroad 1236 (Thrall Manufacturing Company 1967)	Western Pacific Railroad Museum
A Thrall all-door boxcar		
Caboose	Burlington & Missouri River 10 (Wells & French 1878)	Oklahoma Railroad Museum
An ancient caboose built by a very early car builder.		
Disconnects	Rayonier Inc. 3 sets (Russell Wheel & Foundry 1905)	Northwest Railway Museum
Disconnects	Rayonier Inc. (Seattle Car Mfg. Co. 1912)	Northwest Railway Museum
Disconnects	Rayonier Inc. 5 sets (Nisqually-Russel Car & Locomotive Works 1916)	Northwest Railway Museum
Disconnects	L E White Lumber (L E White Lumber)	California State Railroad Museum
Logging disconnect cars (essentially disconnected rail trucks used to carry logs)		

Type	Item	Museum
Flatcar	American Electric Power 1002	Virginia Museum of Transportation
Flatcar	Pennsylvania Railroad 470245 (Pennsylvania Railroad 1952)	Railroaders Memorial Museum
Heavy duty flatcars. AEP 1002 has twelve axles and a capacity of 275 tons. PRR 470245 (known to the railroad employees as the "Queen Mary") is a sixteen-axle car with a capacity of 250 tons.		
Hopper	Baltimore & Ohio 23001 and 23002 (Baltimore & Ohio 1883)	B&O Railroad Museum
These two cars are "pot" hoppers. They consist of iron pots mounted on a railroad chassis.		
Hot metal car	Youngstown Sheet & Tube 21 and 23	Mahoning Valley Railroad Museum
Hot metal car	Unknown Road	Mahoning Valley Railroad Museum
Ingot mold car	Sharon Steel 235	Mahoning Valley Railroad Museum
Slag car	Youngstown Sheet & Tube 17	Mahoning Valley Railroad Museum
Slag car	US Steel 6	Lake Superior Railroad Museum
A selection of steel-industry cars that are almost never seen by the public		
Reefer	J R Simplot Company 5021 (Pacific Car & Foundry 1968)	Western Pacific Railroad Museum
A very unusual cryogenic reefer		
Stock	Poultry Transportation Company 423 (Poultry Car Company 1921)	St. Louis Museum of Transportation
Possibly the rarest of stock cars, this one was designed to haul poultry		
Tank	Bordens 520 (MDC ? 1935)	Illinois Railway Museum
A streamlined milk tank car also known as a butter dish car, believed to be the only survivor of its kind		
Tank	US Department of the Interior 1202 (1962)	Gold Coast Railroad Museum
An unusual helium tank car. The helium is transported in a series of high-pressure cylinders running the length of the car		

Type	Item	Museum
Tank	General American Transportation 96500 (General American Transportation 1965)	St. Louis Museum of Transportation
At 97 feet long, the world's largest tank car		
Non-revenue Equipment		
Crane	Grand Central Terminal GCT-1 (Industrial Crane Works 1914)	Danbury Railway Museum
A very unusual double-ended wrecking crane designed for use in the tunnels approaching Grand Central terminal where space is severely limited		
Instruction car	Norfolk & Western 401	Mad River & NKP Museum
A relatively modern high-cube boxcar modified for use as a classroom		
Clearance Car	Baltimore & Ohio CE-15 (Baltimore & Ohio 1904)	B&O Railroad Museum
A car designed to measure clearances along the right of way		
Torch Car	US Olympics Unknown (2001)	Utah State Railroad Museum
A flat car custom-converted in 2001 to carry the Olympic torch for the 2002 Salt Lake City Olympics		
Rotary plow	Montreal Tramways 5 (1910)	Shore Line Trolley Museum
A rare electric rotary snowplow		
Substation	Sacramento Northern 1 (Sacramento Northern 1920)	Western Railway Museum
A portable substation. Several exist in museums but this one is actually used to power the railroad.		
Track geometry car	Union Pacific EC-1 (Plasser American 1974)	California State Railroad Museum
A relatively modern track geometry car		
Hi-railer	Sierra Railway 8 (Ford Motor Co)	Railtown 1897 State Historic Park
Hi-railer	Sandy River and Rangeley Lakes Railroad (Ford 1925)	Maine Narrow Gauge Railroad & Museum
Hi-railer	Maryland & Pennsylvania 101 (Buick 1937)	B&O Railroad Museum
Hi-railer	Chicago Milwaukee St. Paul & Pacific (Milwaukee Road) 30 (Dodge 1947)	Mid-Continent Railway Museum

Type	Item	Museum
Hi-railer	Erie Mining Company 8440 (Pontiac 1958)	Lake Superior Railroad Museum
A selection of hi-railers (automobiles modified to run on rails)		
Traction Equipment		
Cable	Chicago City Railway 209 (Chicago Surface Lines 1934)	Illinois Railway Museum
Probably the only surviving car from the once-extensive Chicago cable car lines		
Horsecar	North Chicago Street Railroad 8 (John Stevenson Car Company 1859)	Illinois Railway Museum
Horsecar	Citizens Street Railway 69 (1869)	Indiana Transportation Museum
Two ancient horse-drawn cars from the days before electrification		
Inter-urban	Illinois Terminal Railroad 504 (American Car & Foundry Company 1910)	Illinois Railway Museum
Inter-urban	Chicago North Shore & Milwaukee 415 (Cincinnati Car Company 1926)	Seashore Trolley Museum
A rare interurban diner and an even more rare sleeper		
Inter-urban	Key System 167 (Bethlehem Steel 1937)	Orange Empire Railroad Museum
Inter-urban	Key System 182, 186 and 187 (1939)	Western Railway Museum
Four sets of the distinctive Key System articulated bridge cars		
Inter-urban	Philadelphia Suburban Transit Liberty Liner (St Louis Car Company 1941)	Rockhill Trolley Museum
Inter-urban	Chicago North Shore & Milwaukee 801 (St Louis Car Company 1941)	Illinois Railway Museum
High speed interurban Electroliner trains designed for service between Chicago and Milwaukee. In 1963 the two sets were sold to Philadelphia Suburban Transit and became Liberty Liners.		
Rapid Transit	New York Elevated Railroad 41 (1878)	Shore Line Trolley Museum
A money car, used on the New York elevated railways to retrieve cash from the token-sellers		

Type	Item	Museum
Rapid Transit	US Department of Transportation SOAC1 and SOAC2 (St Louis Car Company 1972)	Seashore Trolley Museum
Experimental rapid transit cars. The last cars produced by St Louis Car Company.		

Acknowledgements

This book could not have been written without the internet as much of the information contained here came from the museums' web sites. But not all museum web sites include all of the information necessary. Direct contact with many museums was necessary to flesh out details and thanks are due to the busy volunteers and employees who took the time to respond to requests. In particular, we would like to acknowledge the help of the following people:

- Robert Barcus (Hoosier Valley Railroad Museum)
- Bart Barton (Arizona Railway Museum)
- Mark Bassett (Nevada Northern Railway Museum)
- Ken Buehler (Lake Superior Railroad Museum)
- Tom Carter (Western Pacific Railroad Museum)
- Sandi Cobb (Galveston Railroad Museum)
- Amanda Felix (Utah State Railroad Museum)
- Neil Frasca (Mahoning Valley Railroad Heritage Association)
- Jim Garnett (Heart of Dixie Railroad Museum)
- Hope Banner Graby (Strasburg Rail Road)
- William Gray (Whitewater Valley Railroad)
- Nancy Hall (Maine Narrow Gauge Railroad & Museum)
- Stan Hall (Oklahoma Railway Museum)
- Michael Hall (Gold Coast Railroad Museum)
- Wendell Huffman (Nevada State Railroad Museum)
- Robin Hume (National New York Central Railroad Museum)
- Tim Hyde (Railway Museum of Greater Cincinnati)
- Matt Isaacks (Colorado Railroad Museum)
- Martha Jackson (North Carolina Transportation Museum)
- Patricia Knight (Georgia State Railroad Museum)
- Phil Kohlmetz (Western Railway Museum)
- Lynn Kustes (Kentucky Railway Museum)
- Daniel Liedtke (National Railroad Museum)

- Pat McKnight (Steamtown National Historic Site)
- Barbara Morrow (Heart of Dixie Railroad Museum)
- Kellie Murphy (Museum of the American Railroad)
- Rick Olsen (Indiana Railway Museum)
- Dave Overton (National New York Central Railroad Museum)
- John Penfield (Bluegrass Railroad Museum)
- Dick Pennick (Pacific Southwest Railroad Museum)
- Craig Presler (Indiana Transportation Museum)
- Jamie Reid (Southeastern Railway Museum)
- Taylor Rush (Sumpter Valley Railroad)
- Joel Salomon (Rockhill Trolley Museum)
- Dave Shackelford (B&O Railway Museum)
- Walt Stoner (Northern Ohio Railway Museum)
- Maria Strohm (Railroaders Memorial Museum)
- Rodger Stroup (South Carolina Railroad Museum)
- Carolyn Taylor (Danbury Railway Museum)
- Tim Tennant (Cumbres & Toltec Scenic Railroad)
- Amanda Vance (Galveston Railroad Museum)
- Brian Wise (Mount Rainier Scenic Railroad)
- Kyle Wyatt (California State Railroad Museum)

Credits

Photo and illustration credits are as follows. All uncredited photos were taken by the author.

- Page 6, Railroad Magazine cover, used by permission of Carstens Publications, Inc.
- Page 53, New York, New Haven & Hartford 673 by Carolyn Taylor courtesy of the Danbury Railway Museum.
- Page 55, Philadelphia and West Chester Traction Car 78 by N2xjk at en.wikipedia licensed under the GNU Free Documentation License, Version 1.2
- Page 57, Strasburg 475 courtesy of the Strasburg Rail Road
- Page 61, Seaboard Air Lines number 6300 courtesy of the Gold Coast Railroad Museum
- Page 72, Canadian National number 6789 by aka Kath licensed under the Creative Commons Attribution 2.0 Generic license via Wikimedia
- Page 81, Sumpter Valley numbers 8 and 19 courtesy of the Sumpter Valley Railroad
- Page 86, Monson number 4, by Dan Crow used under the terms of the GNU Free Documentation License via Wikimedia